The Trumpet Blast

Removing the Veil from the
Advent of the Promised One

Minneapolis

SECOND EDITION DECEMBER 2022
The Trumpet Blast: Removing the Veil from the
Advent of the Promised One

10 9 8 7 6 5 4 3 2

ISBN: 978-1-959770-51-0

Cover and interior design: Gary Lindberg

Cover art: Ora Simcha Hadassah
Cover calligraphy: Burhan Zahrai

The calligraphy on the cover depicts "Yá
Alláhu'l-Mustag͟háth," an invocation of the name of God
in the writings of the Báb translated as "O Thou God
Who art invoked."

The Trumpet Blast

Removing the Veil from the
Advent of the Promised One

Roya Akhavan, Ph.D.

Minneapolis

For the love of truth

Also by Roya Akhavan

Peace for Our Planet: A New Approach

Table of Contents

Introduction

Religious prophecies throughout history have converged on a common expectation; the advent of a world redeemer who will fulfill the ultimate destiny of humankind. Variously referred to as the Day of Judgment, the Day of Resurrection, or the End Times, this advent is expected to set in motion unprecedented upheavals as the Promised One takes charge of restoring justice to the world and rewarding the faithful with eternal life.

Visible expectations of an imminent fulfillment of these prophecies began to emerge in various parts of the world during the nineteenth century and led to the formation of a number of messianic movements across the planet, among them the Shaykhí movement, which heralded the Revelation of the Báb.

This book is written to illuminate the station of Ṭáhirih, one of the Báb's leading disciples, as the Trumpeter of the Day of Resurrection and the Remover of the Veil from the advent of the Promised One.

Although several historically accurate books have been written about Ṭáhirih's life and leadership, a reductionistic image of her as a woman who removed her veil as a gesture of emancipation for women continues to persist in the public's imagination. This reductionistic image has, in turn, prevented a befitting understanding of Ṭáhirih 's mission and station in human history.

This book seeks to contribute to a deeper understanding of Ṭáhirih's station by presenting an analysis of a number of relevant topics that have remained largely unaddressed in previous literature. One of the most important among these is the symbolic significance of the "veil" as a prominent motif in Ṭáhirih 's poetic and scholarly discourse and its connection to key concepts in the writings of the Báb and Bahá'u'lláh. Another area of paucity is an analysis of the many unique features that distinguish Ṭáhirih's leadership from all other key figures within the Bábí movement. These include, but are not limited to, the mystical capacities that enabled Ṭáhirih to independently recognize the stations of the Báb and Bahá'u'lláh and the guidance she received from them as she engaged in the process of progressively unveiling the true nature of the Báb's Revelation.

This book is organized into four parts.

Part one will provide a historical context for studying the life, discourse, and station of Ṭáhirih. It will set the stage for understanding the messianic expectations that swept across the world in the mid-nineteenth century, introduce the nature of the challenge posed to the prevailing Islamic orthodoxy by the Shaykhí movement, and provide a brief history of the Twin Revelations of the Báb and Bahá'u'lláh.

Part two will present a concise overview of the life of Ṭáhirih, with special emphasis on providing a cohesive narrative that maintains the focus on the most significant aspects of Ṭáhirih's life and leadership in the Bábí movement.

Part three will seek to open new vistas for understanding the universal vision that animated Ṭáhirih's heroic actions by presenting an analysis of her discourse. In particular, we will focus on Ṭáhirih's symbolic use of the imagery of the "veil" in the context of her expositions on the overarching theme of the progressive revelation of divine truth to humanity. In addition, we will examine the heuristic correspondence in the use of the symbolism of the "veil" in the discourse of Ṭáhirih and the writings of the Báb and Bahá'u'lláh. A primary purpose of this analysis is to illuminate Ṭáhirih's unique and prominent station as a leader who progressively removed the veils from the claims of the Báb in accordance with her visionary knowledge of the circumstances of the Faith.

Part four of the book will bring together the body of evidence regarding Ṭáhirih's significance in human and religious history with an emphasis on the insights gleaned from her own discourse as well as the authoritative writings of the Báb, Bahá'u'lláh, 'Abdu'l-Bahá, and Shoghi Effendi.

Part 1:
The Historical Context

The 19th century was a pivotal period in human history when an exponential rise in technological advancements and social innovations began to revolutionize every aspect of human life. Soon after the sending of the first telegram on May 24, 1844, almost all charts of human activity, whether in the scientific or the social realm, began to move from a nearly horizontal to a nearly vertical position. Unprecedented technological inventions began to connect diverse peoples across the planet in a common web of communication, sparking a growing consciousness of humanity's oneness and interdependence. In the social arena, a new urgency began to emerge about the need to ensure equality of rights for all human beings, leading to a sharp rise in the number of laws enacted against slavery and the first stirrings of action toward gender equality. Peace and social justice began to take on increasing prominence as human ideals, exemplified in the spontaneous formation of more than 400 grassroots peace societies in the second half of the century, as well as the first ever gathering of heads of state at the Hague in 1899 to discuss innovative procedures for peaceful resolution, rather than bloody settlement, of international disputes.

Concurrent with these scientific, social, and political transformations, messianic expectations began to stir across the planet. For centuries, the expectation for the coming of a world redeemer had remained a common element of belief among the world's major religions. The Jews awaited the coming of the Messiah; Christians awaited the Second Coming of Christ; Sunni Muslims awaited the coming of the Mahdi; Shia Muslims expected the appearance of the Hidden Twelfth Imám; Hindus awaited the return of Krishna; Buddhists anticipated the Maitreya; and Zoroastrians awaited the Saoshyant.[1] Yet, throughout the ages, few people actually expected to see

---

1   Rosen, *Founders of Faith*, 327.

these prophecies come true during their lifetime. This contradiction between the widespread internalization of such beliefs and the absence of a real expectation of their realization was carefully managed by the ecclesiastical leaders who were generally not inclined to promote messianic or millenarian expectations because of the direct threat that it would pose to their own authority and power. Nevertheless, visible expectations of an imminent return of the Promised One began to emerge in the 1830's and 1840's, notably among the Millerites and German Templers in the West, and the Shia Muslims in the East.

According to the Biblical prophecies in the Book of Revelation, the return of Christ on the Day of Resurrection was expected to be accompanied by catastrophic upheavals, commonly referred to as the Apocalypse. (It is interesting to note that "apocalypse" is the Greek word for "lifting the veil"). In addition, a number of Biblical prophecies depicted this advent as a physical descent by Christ on a cloud from heaven.

> For the Lord himself will descend
> from heaven with a cry of command,
> with the voice of an archangel, and
> with the sound of the trumpet of God.

And the dead in Christ will rise first.
Then we who are alive, who are left,
will be caught up together with them
in the clouds to meet the Lord in the
air, and so we will always be with the
Lord.[2]

One of the most notable messianic movements of the nineteenth century was the Millerite
movement led by William Miller (1782-1849),
a Baptist lay preacher from northeastern New
York. Based on his years of intensive study of
the Bible prophecies, and Daniel's 2,300-day
prophecy in particular, Miller had come to the
conclusion that the return of Christ was going
to take place sometime between March 21,1843
and March 21,1844 and had begun to teach that
the Second Coming of Christ was at hand. Thousands of people accepted Miller's predictions and
began to prepare for the Second Coming. When
Christ did not descend as expected, another
Millerite preacher, Samuel Snow, offered what
he believed to be a corrected calculation, extend-
ing the date of the prophecy to October 22, 1844.
The absence of a physical appearance by Christ
on the appointed day led to what has come to

2   Thessalonians, 4:13-18.

be known as the "Great Disappointment" of the Millerites.

During the same period and on the other side of the Atlantic, Christopher Hoffmann (1815-1885), a disillusioned German politician turned missionary, was engaged in efforts to create a true Christian community in preparation for the prophesied return of Christ and rebuilding of the temple in Jerusalem. Hoffman and his compatriots founded the German Templer Society in 1861 and began to encourage their coreligionists to sell their earthly possessions and move to the foothills of Mount Carmel in Haifa (then in Palestine) to await the return of Christ on God's holy mountain. The homes built as part of the Templer Colony on the foothills of Mount Carmel can be identified today by the statement "Der Herr ist nahe" (The Lord is near) engraved above each entrance. In the decades that followed, the absence of a physical descent by Christ, coupled with the aftermath of Germany's involvement in the two World Wars, led to the dissipation of the Templer movement.

Concurrent with these messianic movements in the West, a millenarian school of thought was developing on the other side of the world in Karbila, a major center of Shia religious influence in

Iraq. Named after its founder, Shaykh Ahmad Ahsá'í (1743-1828) and further developed by his successor, Sayyid Kázim Rashtí (1793-1843), this new strand in Shia thought came to be known as the Shaykhí school. Despite fierce opposition from orthodox Shia ecclesiastics, the Shaykhí movement, as originally conceived by its founders, succeeded in paving the way for an ultimate fulfillment of its expectations in the person of Siyyid 'Alí Muhammad Shírází, the Báb.

The Shaykhí school was born at a time when the Shia scholars of religious law, known as the 'ulamá, were engaged in consolidating their power in the shrine cities of Iraq and Shia strongholds in Iran. For several centuries, the Shia 'ulamá had held a high level of charismatic authority in Islamic societies. This authority was based on the 'ulamá's claim to be representatives of the Twelfth Imám,[3] who was believed to have gone into concealment in the year 260 A.H. and was expected to return on the Day of Resurrection. The 'ulamá had further succeeded in progressively formalizing their religious learning and had thus arrogated to themselves the authority to render legal judgments based on their abil-

3   Imám Muhammad Ibn Hasan.

ity to interpret religious law (sharí'á). By the
early nineteenth century, the orthodox 'ulamá,
known as the Usúlí mujtahids, had firmly established themselves as a powerful class of ecclesiastics within a hierarchy based on professional
education, demonstrable knowledge of religious
jurisprudence, and licensing (ijtihád). In addition
to their judicial authority, the Usúlí mujtahids
wielded considerable social and economic power
through their leadership positions in mosques
and religious schools as well as their ability to
collect charitable contributions mandated by
Islamic law.[4]

The entrenched power enjoyed by the
Usúlí mujtahids set them on an inevitable col-
lision course with the emerging Shaykhí school.
Although Shaykh Ahmad Ahsá'í was himself a
licensed mujtahid, his teachings proved increasingly antithetical to the positions held by the
Usúlí 'ulamá. As a mystic with frequent spiritual
experiences and visions of the Imáms, Shaykh
Ahmad believed that, in order to function as
an authoritative deputy of the Hidden Imám, it
was necessary to go beyond developing powers of logical reasoning to attain spiritual vision

---

4   According to Islamic law, the believers are obligated to
     contribute one-fifth (*khums*) of their income to charity.

through revelatory experience.[5] This assertion fundamentally challenged the Usúlí mujtahids' claim to their status based on religious knowledge and learned reasoning.

Another challenge to the prevailing religious orthodoxy arose from S̲h̲ayk̲h̲ Ahmad's redefinition of the meaning and manner of Resurrection. In contrast to the centuries-long depiction of the Day of Resurrection within Islamic circles as a physical raising of dead bodies, S̲h̲ayk̲h̲ Ahmad asserted that the corporeal body, i.e., the dried-up bones of the dead, cannot and will not be resurrected. Rather, it is the "spiritual corpse" of the individual, dwelling in an intermediary realm between the heaven and the earth (*havarqalyá*),[6] that will be called forth and given a new corporeal body on the Day of Resurrection. This intermediary realm of *havarqalyá* was also considered by S̲h̲ayk̲h̲ Ahmad as the plane where visionary encounters between the Hidden Imám and his true deputies took place.[7]

---

5   Amanat, *The Early Years of the Bábí Movement*, 32.

6   Rafati, 108. Note: The more recent iterations by other authors refer to this concept as *húrqalya*.

7   Amanat, *The Early Years of the Bábí Movement*, 42. Note: This new conceptualization also redefined the fourth pillar of Shia Islam, i.e., the deputyship of the Imáms, and replaced it with the concept of the "perfect Shia;" one

Perhaps the most significant challenge posed by the Shaykhí school to the entire Usúlí ecclesiastical structure was Shaykh Ahmad's prediction that the appearance of the Hidden Imám was at hand. As deputies of the Hidden Imám, the 'ulamá were allowed to hold authority only in the Imám's absence and would cease to wield any power upon his return.[8] The propagation of such a millenarian expectation was thus antithetical to the very reason for existence of the Shia clerical class.

Although Shaykh Ahmad refrained from an open pronouncement regarding the exact timing of the Hidden Imám's appearance, he is reported to have alluded to an Islamic tradition attributed to Imám Ja'far Sádiq, which states that the Qá'im will appear in "the year sixty."[9] This is a reference to the year 1260 A.H. (one thousand years after the Hidden Imám's occultation) and coincides with 1844 in the Gregorian calendar.

After his death in 1828, Shaykh Ahmad was succeeded by one of his most prominent students, Sayyid Kázim Rashtí. In addition to

---

whose visionary experiences would render him as the true deputy of the Hidden Imám.

8   Smith, 23.

9   Amanat, *The Early Years of the Bábí Movement*, 41.

expanding the philosophical foundations of Shaykhí thought, Sayyid Kázim's teachings intensified the movement's millenarian character. Among the Sayyid's important doctrinal contributions was his conceptualization of prophethood as a cyclical phenomenon. He taught that the old prophetic cycle, characterized by a primary focus on "exteriors," or observing outward rituals (*zaváhir*), had come to an end, and it was now time for a new cycle of progress focused on "interiors," or inner spiritual truths (*bavátin*), to begin. He regarded the outpourings of divine truth and the forward march of human progress as interrelated processes and prophesied about an imminent age of "maturity" for humankind when a new cycle of divine revelation would "unveil the secrets" destined to perfect the capacities of the human spirit.[10]

Shortly before his death, Sayyid Kázim began to tell his students that the Qá'im was already present in the world, urging them to set out to find Him.

> O my beloved companions! . . .It is incumbent upon you to renounce all comfort, all earthly possessions and kindred, in your quest of Him who is

---

10   Amanat, *The Early Years of the Bábí Movement*, 43-44.

the Desire of yours and of mine. . .
Such ones amongst you must neither
falter nor feel dismayed. For soon
after the first trumpet-blast which is to
smite the earth with extermination and
death, there shall be sounded again yet
another call, at which all things will be
quickened and revived. . . Verily I say,
after the Qá'im the Qayyúm will be
made manifest.[11]

In view of the imminence of the advent of
the Qá'im, Sayyid Kázim refused to appoint a
formal successor. Instead, he asked one of his
prominent students, Mullá Hasan Gawhar, to
take temporary charge, saying: "The Cause will
be manifest in another thirty weeks,"[12] a date that
would coincide with the last week of May 1844.

One of the first among Sayyid Kázim's students to heed his call to set out on a search for the
Qá'im was Mullá Husayn Bushrú'í. On Febru-
ary 22, 1844, Mullá Husayn went to the Al-Kúfa
Mosque in Najaf (a shrine city in Iraq) to engage in
a forty-day period of fasting and prayer in prepara-

---

11   Nabíl, *The Dawn Breakers,* 40-41. It is notable that Sayyid
      Kázim here makes reference to the successive revelations
      of the Báb and Bahá'u'lláh.
12   MacEoin, *From Shaykhísm to Bábísm,* 117.

tion for his search. Several other of Sayyid Kázim's students joined him in this retreat shortly thereafter.

Guided by a reference in the Islamic Hadíth to the province of Fars in Iran as the place of the Qá'im's return,[13] as well as an irresistible sense of spiritual attraction, Mullá Husayn set out in the direction of Fars and directed his steps toward Shiraz. Upon arrival, he found the Báb waiting for him at the city gate and accepted His invitation to accompany Him to his home. During the ensuing conversation, which occurred in evening of May 22, 1844, the Báb began to reveal a commentary on the Qur'ánic Súra of Joseph[14] in fulfillment of prophecy, leading Mullá Husayn to recognize the Báb as the object of his quest.

The Báb asked Mullá Husayn to conceal the news of His appearance until seventeen other souls had found him as a result of their own independent search. Once this process was completed,

---

13   Mohammad Hoseini, *Hazrat-i-Ṭáhirih*, 187.

14   This lengthy commentary, entitled the *Qayyúmu'l-Asmá*, was completed in forty days. In addition to extensive commentaries on each of the 111 verses of the Súra of Joseph, the Báb, in essence, interprets the story of Joseph as a symbolic depiction of the dynamics of humanity's search for the Countenance of the Divine Beloved, fulfilled in the revelations of the Báb and Bahá'u'lláh. See Saiedi, *Gate of the Heart,* 30.

the Báb bestowed upon these eighteen early disciples a special station as the *sábiqún* (those who have "preceded in faith"), a term associated with the early disciples of Prophet Muhammad. Later, in the *Persian Bayán*, the Báb referred to them by a new title; the Letters of the Living.[15]

The Báb's disciples fanned throughout Iran and Iraq and began to teach His message, attracting large numbers of followers to the new Faith. Many who accepted the Báb during the early years of His declaration understood the Báb's station as a Gate to the Hidden Imám, and not as the Imám himself. This was, in large part, due to the fact that the Báb chose to unveil His true station in stages in order to reduce the level of shock that a simultaneous announcement of the advent of the Qá'im, the Day of Resurrection, and a completely New Dispensation, would have generated. Despite the gradual unveiling of His station, the Báb was immediately opposed by both the ecclesiastical and governmental authorities in Iran and spent the last three years of His ministry as a prisoner until his execution in Tabriz on July 9, 1850.

Between 1844 and 1847, the Báb's writings

---

15   Saiedi, 240.

17

alluded to His true station in veiled and symbolic language. However, shortly after His arrival in the prison of Maku around July 1847, He began to write His most important doctrinal work, the *Persian Bayán*, in which He proclaimed His station as a new Manifestation of God with teachings and laws that abrogated the Islamic Dispensation.[16] He also revealed that the primary purpose of His Dispensation was to serve as the Gate to a Manifestation greater than himself, "Him whom God shall make manifest," and alluded to the timing as well as the name of the next Manifestation.

The Báb's writings were quite specific regarding the "year nine" as the year of the next Manifestation's appearance, as in the following verses: "In the year nine, ye shall attain to all good," and again, "In the year nine, ye will attain unto the presence of God."[17] Elsewhere, the Báb beseeches Him Whom God shall make manifest to conceal Himself until nineteen years have passed from His own Declaration:

> I, indeed, beg to address Him Whom
> God shall make manifest, by thy leave

16   Saiedi, *Gate of the Heart*, 19.
17   Shoghi Effendi, *God Passes By*, 29.

in these words: '. . . do Thou grant a respite of nineteen years as a token of Thy favor so that those who have embraced this Cause may be graciously rewarded by Thee.'[18]

Despite referring to Himself as the Most Great Name in some texts, the Báb asserts that the ultimate realization of the Most Great Name is "Bahá"[19] and commands the Bábís to prepare to humble themselves before Him:

> When the Daystar of Bahá will shine resplendent above the horizon of eternity it is incumbent upon you to present yourselves before His Throne.[20]

In addition to heralding the advent of Him Whom God shall make manifest, the Báb's writings set forth spiritually and sociologically revolutionary concepts. One of the Báb's most revolutionary teachings was the assertion that all human beings are sacred handiworks of God and have been created with the potential to reflect His attributes. Therefore, all human beings must be given equal rights and opportunities to ful-

---

18   The Báb, *Selections from the Writings of the Báb*, 1:2:4.

19   Saiedi, *Gate of the Heart*, 106.

20   The Báb, *Selections from the Writings of the Báb*, 6:14:1.

fill their highest potential regardless of gender, background, position, or class. In a world built on hierarchy and autocratic rule whether in religious, social, or political arenas, the Báb's teachings depicted all human beings, regardless of their social class, as equally noble emanations of the same divine reality.[21] This concept alone, among the Báb's many other revolutionary teachings, delegitimized all systems of domination and subjugation based on exertion of power by one human being over another.

Furthermore, the Báb taught that the spiritual energies released into the world by the new outpourings of divine truth in each age infuse fresh capacities in all beings and propel them toward new heights of progress and perfection. From that perspective, the synchronicity between the Báb's transformative vision for humanity and the emergence of a new social consciousness about dignity and rights for all human beings in the nineteenth century is not surprising.

As already mentioned, not only did the Báb reveal a new Dispensation, He also announced that His mission was to prepare the world for One

---

21 For additional insights, see the series of talks by Nader Saiedi on the *Persian Bayán*, available on the Worldwide Web.

greater than Himself. It is clear from historical accounts, furthermore, that the Báb was already aware of the identity of Him Whom God shall make manifest. On the eve of His departure on pilgrimage to Mecca and Medina in fulfillment of prophecy, the Báb summoned Mullá Husayn and asked him to arise to teach His Cause throughout Iran. He also gave him special instructions to travel to Tehran to find a "a secret" that lay hidden in that city:

> Beseech almighty Providence that He
> may graciously enable you to attain,
> in that capital, the seat of true sover-
> eignty and to enter the mansion of the
> Beloved. A secret lies hidden in that
> city. When made manifest, it shall turn
> the earth into paradise. My hope is
> that you may partake of its grace and
> recognize its splendor.[22]

After stops in Isfahan, Kashan, and Qum, Mullá Husayn set out toward Tehran on yet another spiritual quest, this one at the command of the Báb. While in Tehran, he met a youth who told him about a distinguished personage of noble lineage by the name of Mirzá

---

22   Nabíl, *The Dawn Breakers*, 86.

Husayn 'Alí Núrí, known for his deep knowledge, disinterest in worldly affairs, and dedication to the cause of the poor. Recognizing the object of his quest in that description, Mullá Husayn gave the youth a scroll containing a tablet from the Báb and asked him to deliver it to the noble personage he had spoken of. When the scroll was delivered to Mírzá Husayn 'Alí the next day, he immediately recognized its contents as having the same "Divine Origin"[23] as the Qur'án. He became a believer in the Báb and went on to take up the mantle of leadership in the Bábí Cause. Although the Báb and Mírzá Husayn 'Alí (whom from here on we shall refer to as Bahá'u'lláh) never met in person, they maintained close contact through correspondence until the Báb's martyrdom in July 1850. Prior to his execution, the Báb arranged for His pens, seals, and writings to be delivered to Bahá'u'lláh.

Even after the Báb's execution in July 1850, His followers continued to sustain severe persecution at the hands of religious and civic authorities in Iran. In 1852, Bahá'u'lláh was arrested and imprisoned, along with dozens of

---

23   Nabíl, 106.

other Bábís, in an underground dungeon in Tehran known as the Black Pit. In the course of that confinement, Bahá'u'lláh had a vision in which a "Maiden," whom He describes as "the embodiment of the remembrance of the Name of My Lord,"[24] revealed to Him that He was the Manifestation promised by the Báb.

After four months in the Black Pit, Bahá'u'lláh was banished to Baghdad as a prisoner of the Persian and Ottoman Empires. During the next ten years, while concealing His true station, Bahá'u'lláh continued to lead the Bábí community in Baghdad and revealed a number of important works, including *The Book of Certitude.* Bahá'u'lláh's open declaration of His mission as a new Manifestation occurred in April 1863, in the course of a 12-day period of encampment on the eve of His exile to Constantinople.

After a four-month stay in Constantinople, Bahá'u'lláh and His family were exiled to Adrianople. It was in Adrianople that Bahá'u'lláh began the process of unequivocally proclaiming the universal nature of His mission by addressing a series of Tablets to all major kings and rulers of the time, including the Ottoman King and the King of Persia.[25]

---

24   Bahá'u'lláh, *Summons of the Lord of Hosts,* 5.
25   Beginning in 1867 in Adrianople and continuing after His arrival in the prison city of Akka, Bahá'u'lláh addressed

From Adrianople, Bahá'u'lláh was banished to the fortress of Akka, a prison city in the Ottoman territory in Palestine. After being released from that prison, He lived under house arrest in Palestine until His passing in 1892. In one of the last years of His earthly life, Bahá'u'lláh made a short visit to Haifa and pitched His tent on Mount Carmel. During that visit, He designated the spot where the remains of the Báb were to be buried.

Bahá'u'lláh passed away on May 29, 1892, at the Mansion of Bahjí in the outskirts of Akka and was buried in a nearby structure. Decades after His execution in Tabriz, the Báb's remains were finally brought to the Holy Land and on March 21, 1909 His casket was interned on the spot previously designated by Bahá'u'lláh on Mount Carmel.

As reflected in this brief overview, the nineteenth century marked a period of unprecedented transformation in the life of humanity as a result of the blossoming of new and revolutionary spiritual visions as well as rapidly advancing scientific discoveries and social innovations. Perhaps

---

a series of tablets to the kings and rulers of the time, including Emperor Napoleon III, Queen Victoria, Kaiser Wilhelm, Tsar Alexander II, Emperor Franz Joseph, Pope Pius IX, Sultan 'Abdu'l-Aziz, and Nasiri'd-Din Shah.

the most transformative vision of the nineteenth century was that reflected in the teachings of the Báb. In addition to elevating all human beings to the station of sanctity and declaring the equality of all people, the Báb promulgated the principles of progressive revelation of divine truth and oneness of all Manifestations, underscored the need for every human being to independently investigate the truth, and rejected all ecclesiastic systems of authority and intervention.

Despite the gradual manner in which the Báb revealed His mission, His ministry was characterized by unspeakable suffering as a result of violent opposition to Him and His followers. The opposition to the Bábí Cause arose primarily from the threat that it posed to the established power of the ecclesiastical authorities of the time and was intensified by the dark veils of prejudice and entrenched habit that shut people out from recognizing new truths. In the process of proclaiming the new Faith, many veils needed to be lifted and many outworn mindsets, habits, and rituals cast aside. The primary leadership role in progressively lifting those veils and ultimately proclaiming the true nature of the Báb's Revelation as a new Dispensation was taken up by Ṭáhirih, one of the Báb's foremost Letters of the Living.

Part 2:
The Life Story of Ṭáhirih

Fátimá Zarrín-Táj Baragh̲ání (1814/17-1852),[26] known by her two titles as Qurratu'l-'Ayn and Ṭáhirih, was born in a prominent family in Qazvin, Iran. Ṭáhirih's father, Mullá Sálih, was an erudite Islamic scholar who headed the famous Sálihiyyih school in Qazvin and her mother, Áminih, was also a woman of high learning who taught at the girls' section of the same school.[27]

Ṭáhirih's unique family circumstances provided a hospitable environment for her innate gifts and brilliance to flourish. She mastered Arabic, logic, religious traditions, and the Qur'án at an early

---

26 Ṭáhirih's exact date of birth is not known. The year of her birth is estimated differently by various authors and varies between 1814 and 1817. Also see footnote # 28.

27 Mohammad Hoseini, *Hazrat-i-Ṭáhirih*, 134. Also see, Momen, "Usúlí, Akh̲barí, S̲h̲aykh̲í, Bábí," 327-28.

age and surpassed her peers with such rapidity that her father was compelled to educate her himself.

Despite having been brought up in a home where she was deeply loved and revered, Ṭáhirih could not escape the traditional pressures that compelled her to marry her paternal cousin, Mullá Muhammad, at the age of fourteen. Ṭáhirih's marriage placed her in an oppressive environment dominated not only by her husband but also her father-in-law, Mullá Taqí Baraghání, a prominent Usúlí mujtahid.

Shortly after marriage, Ṭáhirih moved with her husband to Karbila in order for him to further his Islamic studies. During the couple's thirteen-year residence in Karbila,[28] Ṭáhirih became familiar with the Shaykhí school and was immediately attracted to its concepts and teachings.

---

28 If we consider the year 1817 as the correct date for Ṭáhirih's birth, the reported thirteen years of residence in Karbila becomes problematic. This is because adding fourteen (the age at which Ṭáhirih was married) to thirteen years of residence in Karbila makes 27. Adding 27 to 1817 will bring us to 1844 for the date of the couple's return to Qazvin. Yet, we know that Ṭáhirih was already residing back in Qazvin prior to 1843 and had, for some time, been subjected to severe demands by her husband and father-in-law to give up her Shaykhí beliefs. Therefore, we must either accept 1814 as the date of her birth or assume that the couple lived fewer than thirteen years in Karbila.

Evidence suggests that she officially converted to Shaykhísm at the age of nineteen,[29] several years prior to Sayyid Kázim's passing. Although it is unclear whether Ṭáhirih ever personally met Sayyid Kázim in Karbila, she did establish secret correspondence with him and began to write lengthy essays expounding upon and defending Shaykhí ideas. It was in response to one of these brilliant essays that Sayyid Kázim referred to her as Qurratu'l-ʻAyn (solace of the eyes), the title by which she came to be known in the Shaykhí circles. The title of Ṭáhirih (pure) was first bestowed upon her in a letter written by the Báb and was later formalized by Bahá'u'lláh at the Conference of Badasht.

Upon the couple's return to Qazvin with two sons and one daughter, the conditions in Ṭáhirih's extended family became increasingly tense. By then, Ṭáhirih's husband was an Usúlí mujtahid and her father-in-law, Mullá Taqí, who led the Friday prayers, had become the most powerful mujtahid in Qazvin. Both men vehemently opposed the Shaykhí teachings and were violently angered at Ṭáhirih's conversion. Ultimately, the pressures on Ṭáhirih to abandon her

---

29   Mohammad Hoseini, *Hazrat-i-Ṭáhirih*, 173.

spiritual quest became so intense that she had to leave her home and move to her father's house. Ṭáhirih's father, who dearly loved his daughter, made various attempts to mediate, but was unsuccessful.

Ṭáhirih was not the only Shaykhí in her family. Her youngest uncle, Mullá Muhammad 'Alí Baraghání, her sister, Marzíyyih, and her brother-in-law, Mullá Muhammad 'Alí Qazvíní, shared her beliefs. Her maternal cousin, Mullá Javád, who became an early facilitator of her Shaykhí studies, embraced Shaykhísm only to abandon it later.[30]

Burning with a deep love for the truth and having found the object of her spiritual quest in the Shaykhí teachings, Ṭáhirih finally took the bold step in 1843 of leaving Qazvin with her sister and brother-in-law to join Sayyid Kázim's circle in Karbila.[31]

Ṭáhirih and her companions arrived in Sayyid Kázim's house only to learn that he had passed away. Upon meeting Ṭáhirih, the Sayy-

---

30 Amanat, *Resurrection and Renewal*, 297.
31 According to Momen, Ṭáhirih took her daughter along with her to Karbila. See Momen, "Uṣúlí, Akhbári, Shaykhí, Bábí," p. 329. It is widely believed, however, that she was never reunited with her two older sons after leaving Qazvin.

id's wife became an instant devotee and invited her to stay and continue to teach his students. Ṭáhirih's unmatched eloquence, magnetic personality, and masterful knowledge of scripture soon attracted many of the Sayyid's most erudite students to her.[32]

Based on Sayyid Kázim's clear admonitions regarding the nearness of the advent of the Qá'im, Ṭáhirih began to immerse herself in constant prayer and supplication to be able to recognize the Promised One. One night in a dream she saw the Qá'im suspended between the heavens and the earth reciting certain verses. She memorized those verses by writing them down in her notebook upon waking.[33]

During the days when Mullá Husayn and his companions were praying and fasting at the Great Mosque of Kufá, Ṭáhirih was similarly engaged in ardent supplications. Despite her great desire to search for the Qá'im herself, however, it was not possible for her to travel as a lone woman across mountains and roads. Instead, learning that her trusted brother-in-law, Mullá Muhammad 'Alí, was about to embark on such a search, Ṭáhirih wrote a letter professing her faith and asked him to give it to

---

32   Mohammad Hoseini, 184.

33   'Abdu'l-Bahá, *Memorials of the Faithful*, 190.

the Qá'im upon finding Him.[34]

Two months after Mullá Husayn met the Báb in Shiraz and accepted Him as the Promised One, Ṭáhirih's brother-in-law, Mullá Muhammad 'Alí, met and recognized the Báb and presented Ṭáhirih's letter to him. The Báb immediately accepted Ṭáhirih's faith and, in a letter addressed to Ṭáhirih, declared her as one of the Letters of the Living.

When the Báb's first volume of writings, the Commentary on the Súra of Joseph (*Qayyúmu'l-Asmá*), reached Ṭáhirih shortly thereafter, she recognized in its pages the same verses uttered by the Qá'im in her dream. Despite the widespread lack of understanding at the time among believers and non-believers alike of the exact claims of the Báb, Ṭáhirih's earlier revelatory experience combined with her visionary grasp of the allusions in the *Qayyúmu'l-Asmá*, led her to reach certitude in her recognition of the Báb as the Promised Qá'im.

Ṭáhirih's soul-stirring discourse and indomitable spirit had already placed her in a prominent position of leadership among the Shaykhís in Karbila. Now, having recognized the true sta-

---

34   Balyuzi, *The Báb*, 26.

tion of the Báb, years before He Himself chose to openly proclaim it, Ṭáhirih was transformed into a roaring ocean whose mighty force no one could resist. From the first moment of that recognition, she began to conscientiously choreograph her life as one in which every word and action was designed to unveil the truth of the new Revelation.

As a uniquely qualified religious and literary scholar, Ṭáhirih undertook the task of translating the *Qayyúmu'l-Asmá* from the original Arabic into Persian and began to propagate its contents. In her efforts to publicly proclaim the advent of the Báb, Ṭáhirih wrote lengthy dissertations addressed to high-ranking ʻulamá in Karbila, inviting them to embrace the new cause. The direct challenge posed by her audacious proclamations greatly inflamed the ʻulamá, who fiercely rejected her claims and condemned her as a heretic.

The Uṣúlí ʻulamá were not the only group who opposed Ṭáhirih. The challenge her revolutionary interpretations of the Báb's writings presented to the religious status quo also disturbed the conservative Shaykhís and caused great consternation among the Bábís. Unlike the generality of the Bábís, whose vision of the new

Faith continued to remain strongly wedded to the existing laws and traditions of Islam, Ṭáhirih was convinced that the time for the observance of outward rituals had come to an end, and it was now time to seek out the inner mysteries of divine truth.[35]

Among the conservative Bábí leaders who opposed Ṭáhirih was Mullá Ahmad Hisárí, a prominent student of Sayyid Kázim, who disagreed vehemently with Ṭáhirih's proclamations, particularly with the assertion that the advent of the Báb had begun a period of interregnum in which many of the Shia rituals needed to be suspended in preparation for the revelation of a new Cause.[36]

Faced with mounting opposition from all directions in Karbila, Ṭáhirih decided to leave for Kazimayn in August of 1846 for a period of six months to allow for the tumult to subside. Her stay in Kazimayn, however, only served to further spread her fame in the region and large numbers of people began to travel from other nearby cities, including Baghdad, to hear her.

The continued opposition within the Bábí circles to Ṭáhirih's interpretations of the Báb's revelation

---

35   MacEoin, *From Shaykhism to Bábísm*, 184.
36   Amanant, *Resurrection and Renewal*, 304.

prompted Mullá Ahmad Hisárí and another promi-
nent Bábí, Sayyid 'Alí Bi<u>sh</u>r, to join together and send
a letter of complaint to the Báb. Their letter stated that:

> [The Báb] has not abrogated the old
> Sharí'á and did not renew any com-
> mand but increased [observation] of
> the religious injunctions and empha-
> sized [the necessity] of prayer and
> fasting and prohibited smoking and
> now this woman Qurrat al-'Ayn has
> exceeded the limit and abrogated the
> Sharí'á that we inherited from our
> fathers and grandfathers without the
> mandate of his holiness the Exalted
> One [i.e., the Báb.][37]

The Báb's reply, which arrived from Maku in
mid-1847, unequivocally defended Ṭáhirih, mark-
ing the first time He referred to her as Ṭáhirih (pure)
and Saddíqih (truthful/righteous), and stated:

> Concerning what you have inquired
> about that mirror which has purified
> its soul in order to reflect the word by
> which all matters are solved; she is a
> righteous, learned, active, and pure

---

37 Amanat, *Resurrection and Renewal*, 307, quoted from
Baghdadi, 109-10.

woman; and do not dispute al-Tahirah
in her command, for she is aware of the
circumstances of the cause and there is
nothing for you but submission to her,
since it is not destined for you to realize
the truth of her status.[38]

When the Báb's response was read to a
group of seventy Bábís in Kazimayn, Siyyid 'Alí
Bishr and several of his compatriots abandoned
the Faith.[39]

It is clear from Ṭáhirih's own discourse
that, though impatient in revealing the "Hidden
Secret"[40] she had discovered, she consistently
acted in accordance with the Báb's will and only
unveiled what she understood to be in line with
His progressively unfolding claims.[41]

Ṭáhirih returned to Karbila from Kazimayn in late 1846. By then her fame had
spread throughout the holy cities of Iraq and
her devoted followers had come to be known as
the *Qurratíyyih*. Shortly after her return, Ṭáhirih
engaged in one of her most revolutionary sym-

---

38   Ibid.
39   Mohammad Hoseini, 205.
40   The concept of the "Hidden Secret" and its unveiling con-
      stitutes a primary motif in the discourse of Ṭáhirih.
41   MacEoin, 184.

bolic actions. In a highly audacious act on the first of Muharram,[42] the anniversary of the martyrdom of Imám Husayn, Ṭáhirih defied centuries of strict Shia tradition by dressing in colorful clothes and celebrating the birth of the Báb, which falls on the same date. The extraordinary nature of this symbolic act becomes clear when we consider the fact that the martyrdom of Imám Husayn was, and continues to be, deeply reified in the psyche of Shia Muslims as a calamity of unprecedented proportions, strictly observed as an occasion when everyone is expected to wear black and weep, as men march in the streets demonstrating the depth of their mourning in acts of self-mutilation.

In yet another revolutionary act, Ṭáhirih challenged to public debate the clerics who had denounced her written proclamations. This chal-

---

42 According to MacEoin, p. 184, this episode occurred on 1 Muharram 1263/December 1846. It is important to note that Amanat gives the date of 1 Muharram 1845 for this incident; see *Resurrection and Renewal*, p. 305. However, MacEoin states that he has deduced 1846 to be the correct date because Samandar cites this episode as one of the reasons for Ṭáhirih's move to Baghdad. In the context of the research conducted by this author, it would be more plausible to assume that such a revolutionary act by Ṭáhirih would take place at the later date, i.e.,1846, closer in time to the Báb's revelation of the *Persian Bayán*.

lenge embarrassed and humiliated the 'ulamá, who knew full well that they were incapable of responding to her brilliant arguments. Instead of engaging in debate, they submitted complaints to the Chief of Baghdad and the Ottoman government and incited a mob to attack a house they believed to be Ṭáhirih's residence.[43] Ṭáhirih informed the authorities of her actual place of residence and was subsequently placed under house arrest.

After three months, Ṭáhirih petitioned the authorities and was freed from confinement on the condition that she would leave Karbila. She subsequently set out for Baghdad and accepted the invitation of Shaykh Muhammad Shibl, a devoted Bábí, to live at his house. Once again, multitudes of people came to listen to her every day.

During her stay in Baghdad, Ṭáhirih continued to write lengthy letters to the high-ranking 'ulamá of the city. This time, however, she went further by inviting them to *Mubáhilih,* a form of debate in which both sides accept to be struck by God's wrath if they are in error.[44] By resorting to this unprecedented challenge, Ṭáhirih was communicating to the 'ulamá that if they

---

43   Mohammad Hoseini, 199.
44   Amanat, *Resurrection and Renewal*, 308.

remained unwilling to respond to well-argued dissertations, or to engage in public debates, the only other way to settle the issue was for both sides to wager their life and honor to prove the truth of their assertions. Rejecting Ṭáhirih's challenge, the 'ulamá submitted a complaint to Najíb Páshá, the Chief of Baghdad. Not finding any reason to arrest Ṭáhirih, but wishing to curtail her activities, Najíb Páshá ordered Ṭáhirih to move to the home of Ibn-i-Alúsí, the Mufti of Baghdad,[45] where she stayed for two months. Despite Ibn-i-Alúsí's prior antipathy against the Bábís, he was deeply impressed by Ṭáhirih and, in a later account, referred to her as "a wise and decent woman who was unique in virtue."[46] Evidence suggests, furthermore, that as a result of his conversations with Ṭáhirih, Ibn-i-Alúsí had accepted the new faith in his heart, though he did not express his belief publicly for fear of the "Ottoman swords."[47]

At the end of the winter of 1847, a response to the original complaint by the 'ulamá of Kar-

---

45 A Mufti is a high-ranking Islamic scholar authorized to act as a judge. Note: Ṭáhirih's total stay in Baghdad was three months, two of which were spent at the Mufti's house.

46 Quoted in Amanat, 310.

47 Mohammad Hoseini, 201.

bila to the Ottoman government reached Baghdad. It said that Ṭáhirih can be set free as long as she does not stay within the Ottoman territory. Subsequently, Ṭáhirih's family dispatched an envoy to Ibn-i-Alúsí requesting that she be sent back to Qazvin.

Accompanied by about thirty of her Arab and Persian followers, Ṭáhirih set out toward Iran the next day. Throughout her journey from Baghdad to Qazvin, she continued to publicly proclaim the new Faith, converting large numbers of people in each city. In the village of Karand, Ṭáhirih attracted the allegiance of as many as 1200 people from the Ahl-i-Haqq background.[48] Upon arrival in Kermanshah, she issued an invitation for public *Mubáhilih* to the city's Grand Mujtahid, 'Abdu'lláh Bihbahání. Fearful and angry, the Grand Mujtahid left the city and hid himself. He then wrote a letter of complaint to Ṭáhirih's father and uncle and went on to incite the local army commander to send his soldiers to raid Ṭáhirih's residence and attack her retinue.[49] Undaunted by this violent attack, Ṭáhirih wrote a letter admonishing the authorities and asked for the

---

48   Quoted in Amanat, 1989, Baghdadi, 116.
49   Mohammad Hoseini, 216.

return of the looted belongings.

Ṭáhirih's next stop on her journey back to Qazvin was Hamadan, where she continued to hold public meetings and win devoted followers, including many among the highest religious, social, and governmental ranks. She also sent a bold letter to the Head Mujtahid of the city, proclaiming the new Faith. Her letter so inflamed the Mujtahid that he had the bearer of the letter, Mullá Ibráhím Mahallátí, beaten to near death and thrown in the street.[50]

After spending two months in Hamadan, Ṭáhirih made preparations to go to Tehran to meet Muhammad Shah, Iran's monarch, with the intent to proclaim the new faith to him in-person. However, she was prevented from making the journey by her brothers who had been sent on a mission to return her to Qazvin.

Upon her arrival at her parental home in Qazvin, Ṭáhirih's husband, Mullá Muhammad, asked her to return to him. Although in the Shia tradition of Islam the right to pronounce divorce belonged only to the husband, who could do so at will, Ṭáhirih announced that she was unilaterally divorcing her husband. She said:

---

50   Ibid, 220.

If your desire had really been to be a
faithful mate and companion to me,
you would have hastened to meet me
in Karbila and would on foot have
guided my howdah all the way to
Qazvin. I would, while journeying
with you, have aroused you from
your sleep of heedlessness and would
have shown you the way of truth. But
this was not to be. Three years have
elapsed since our separation. Neither
in this world nor in the next can I ever
be associated with you. I have cast
you out of my life forever.[51]

Ṭáhirih's blunt refusal to be reunited with her
husband so insulted her father-in-law, Mullá Taqí,
that he became violent and struck her during an
argument. Already known for his fierce opposition
to the Bábí movement, he became ever more ruth-
less in his persecution of the Bábís after that incident. One day, as he was praying in the mosque,
he was fatally stabbed by a Shaykhí sympathizer,
Mírzá "Abdu'lláh, who subsequently fled the
scene. Ṭáhirih was immediately implicated along
with many other Bábís and a massacre ensued. To

---

51   Nabíl, 274.

stop the killing, Mírzá "Abdu'lláh surrendered and confessed to his independently conceived crime. This, however, did little to stop the persecution of the Bábís.

Among those agitating most vehemently against Ṭáhirih was her estranged husband, who continued to blame her for his father's death. Despite having been interrogated and cleared of the charges by the Mayor of Qazvin, Ṭáhirih remained under suspicion of her husband's family. During this time, she spent her days under strict observation tantamount to a house arrest at her father's house, as her husband continued to plead with the Persian government to arrest her. Not succeeding in these efforts, he devised a plan to poison her.[52]

Intuitively aware of her husband's intentions, Ṭáhirih stopped eating any food other than that brought to her secretly by trusted women in the area. She then wrote to her husband, saying:

> 'Fain would they put out God's light
> with their mouths; but God only desireth
> to perfect His light, albeit the infidels
> abhor it.'[53] If my Cause be the Cause of

---

52   Mohammad Hoseini, 245.

53   *Qur'án*, 9:33.

Truth, if the Lord whom I worship be
none other than the one true God, He
will, ere nine days have elapsed, deliver
me from the yoke of your tyranny.
Should He fail to achieve my deliverance, you are free to act as you desire.
You will have irrevocably established
the falsity of my belief.[54]

Informed of the grave dangers surrounding Ṭáhirih, Bahá'u'lláh wrote a letter to her
and asked Áqá Muḥammad Hádí to deliver it
to Ṭáhirih and arrange for her to be rescued and
taken to His house in Tehran. The rescue process
was planned in detail by Bahá'u'lláh.[55] Despite
being under strict observation, Ṭáhirih was able
to leave Qazvin nine days after wagering with
her husband that God would, within nine days,
prepare the means for her freedom.

Astonished by her sudden disappearance,
Ṭáhirih's family, and her husband in particular looked everywhere but could not find her.
Despite the dangers surrounding her, Ṭáhirih
refused to relinquish her activities and continued
to accept visitors and hold discussions during her

---

54 Nabíl, 284.
55 Nabíl, 284-7.

five-day stay at the house of Bahá'u'lláh. As the news of Ṭáhirih's whereabouts began to reach her enemies, Bahá'u'lláh, the son of a Minister himself, arranged for her to move to the home of the Minister of War for greater protection.56

These events coincided with the Báb's confinement in Maku during which He revealed the *Persian Bayán* in preparation for unveiling the full scope of His station as the Promised One. Prior to this formal announcement, and in accordance with Islamic prophecies, the Báb issued a call to his followers to raise the Black Standard and set out toward Khorasan.[57] Although the Báb and Bahá'u'lláh never met in person, they had maintained a continuous flow of communication with each other throughout the Báb's ministry. Having learned of the Báb's intention, Bahá'u'lláh undertook the responsibility of facilitating the dramatic unveiling of the Báb's true station.

Bahá'u'lláh's choice of a gathering place for the believers was the hamlet of Badasht on the border of Mazandaran and Khorasan. Undertak-

---

56   Mohammad Hoseini, 254.

57   The Black Standard is a flag historically used during Islamic uprisings. An Islamic Tradition attributes the following prophecy to Prophet Mohammad: "There will emerge from Khorasan black banners which nothing will repel until they are set up in Jerusalem."

ing all expenses of the conference, he proceeded to rent three gardens in Badasht; one for himself, one for Ṭáhirih, and one for Quddús,[58] with three pavilions surrounding an open field where the other attendees were to set up their tents. Bahá'u'lláh also arranged for Ṭáhirih's journey to Badasht, asking His brother, Mírzá Músá, to serve as her guard.[59]

By mid-June of 1848, eighty-one other Bábís had joined Bahá'u'lláh, Ṭáhirih, and Quddús in Badasht for a conference that lasted twenty-two days. This gathering coincided with the Báb's trial in Tabriz in July 1848, during which He publicly declared His station as the Promised Qá'im.

As described by 'Abdu'l-Bahá in the *Memorials of the Faithful*, during the days of Badasht, Bahá'u'lláh, Quddús, and Ṭáhirih met every night to plan that momentous announcement. Their carefully choreographed process, orchestrated by Bahá'u'lláh and carried out by Ṭáhirih and Quddús, was designed to help prepare the believers for the shock and aston-

---

58   Mullá Muhammad 'Alí Bárfurúshí, known by the title of Quddús, was one of the Báb's most prominent Letters of the Living. An appropriate treatment of his station requires a separate volume.

59   Mohammad Hoseini, 263.

ishment that the announcement of the Day of
Resurrection would generate.[60]

During the first days of the gathering, Ṭáhirih
and Quddús engaged in ongoing debates about the
nature of the Báb's revelation. Soon, the debates
were accompanied by dramatic symbolic actions
that signaled the abrogation of the laws of Islam.
Fáḍil Mázandarání relates the following observa-
tions made by Mullá Ahmad 'Alláqihband:

> During the days of Badasht, Ṭáhirih
> would repeatedly appear among the
> believers and with the eloquence, audac-
> ity, and power characteristic of hers
> would command Quddús to 'gather up
> this spread, as the time for repeating
> verses atop prayer seals has come to
> an end. Now we must get ready for the
> fields of love and sacrifice.'[61]

Despite Bahá'u'lláh's role as the primary
orchestrator of the "pre-conceived"[62] plan
unfolding at Badasht, He remained largely
behind the scenes. Each day, however, he would
reveal a new tablet, which the attendees assumed

---

60   Shoghi Effendi, *God Passes By*, 31.
61   Quoted in Mohammad Hoseini, 271; Provisional transla-
     tion from the original Persian by this author.
62   Shoghi Effendi, *God Passes By*, 32.

to be from the Báb.[63] In addition, Bahá'u'lláh proceeded to bestow a new title upon every believer. It was here that Qurratu'l-'Ayn officially acquired the title of "Ṭáhirih" (previously given to her by the Báb), Mullá Muhammad 'Alí Bárfurúshí was given the title, "Quddús," and Bahá'u'lláh, publicly known as Mírzá Husayn 'Alí Núrí, took up the title of "Bahá."[64]

The climactic announcement of the Day of Resurrection at Badasht required that an appropriate stage be set, with the attendees gathered around the central figures of the drama. On the appointed day, Quddús decided to pay a visit to Bahá'u'lláh, who purportedly was not feeling well. Hearing the news, the other believers also began to gather inside Bahá'u'lláh's pavilion. Shortly thereafter, Muhammad Hassan Qazvíní came into the tent to tell Quddús that Ṭáhirih had asked him to pay her a visit. Quddús refused and said that he no longer wished to have any meetings with Ṭáhirih.

The stage for the dramatic announcement of the New Day was now set. Suddenly, Ṭáhirih rushed into Bahá'u'lláh's tent without a veil and, facing the believers, began to give a rousing

63   Mohammad Hoseini, 271.
64   Shoghi Effendi, 32.

speech on the essential themes of the Qur'án.[65] She then recited a Qur'ánic verse which refers to the gathering of the believers in heaven in the presence of the "potent King."[66] As she did so, she glanced in the direction of Bahá'u'lláh and Quddús, an indication that she was intuitively aware of the station of Bahá'u'lláh.[67] This was followed by Ṭáhirih's dramatic announcement: "This is the sound of the bugle. This is the Trumpet Blast!"[68] thereby proclaiming the fulfillment of the Qur'ánic prophecy regarding the sounding of the "Trumpet" on the Day of Judgment.

Ṭáhirih's apocalyptic proclamations and unveiled appearance so shocked the attendees that many of them fled the scene and took refuge in the abandoned houses nearby. One believer cut his own throat and several others abandoned their belief in the Báb.[69] Undeterred by the commotion, Ṭáhirih continued to address the remaining believers in a voice that resembled revelation of verses: "I am the Word which the Qá'im is to

---

65   Shoghi Effendi, 32.

66   Nabíl, 295.

67   Ṭáhirih's awareness of the station of Bahá'u'lláh is clear in her own written discourse. It has also been confirmed by Bahá'u'lláh. See Parts 3 and 4 in this book.

68   'Abdu'l-Baha, *Memorials of the Faithful*, 202.

69   Mohammad Hoseini, 273.

utter, the Word which shall put to flight the chiefs and nobles of the earth!"[70]

Ṭáhirih's announcement of the Advent of the Qá'im was unequivocally affirmed by Bahá'u'lláh when He asked that the *Súra of the Inevitable*, which depicts the Day of Judgement in the Qur'án, be recited:

> When the Event that must occur will become a reality; Then no (soul) will have denial regarding its happening; It will abase (many) and exalt (many others); When the earth shall be shaken to its depths; And the mountains shall be crushed into atoms; . . . And you shall be sorted out into three classes; Then (there will be) the companions of the right hand. . .; And (there will be) the companions of the left hand. . .; And those foremost (in Faith) will be foremost (in the Hereafter).[71]

After this announcement, the gathering of Badasht continued for several more days. According to Nabíl in the *Dawn Breakers*:

> Each day of that memorable gathering

---

70   Shoghi Effendi, 32-3.

71   Qur'án, 56.1-10

witnessed the abrogation of a new law
and the repudiation of a long-estab-
lished tradition. The veils that guarded
the sanctity of the ordinances of Islam
were sternly rent asunder, and the idols
that had so long claimed the adoration
of their blind worshippers were rudely
demolished. No one knew, however, the
Source whence these bold and defiant
innovations proceeded, no one suspected
the Hand which steadily and unerringly
steered their course.[72]

The remaining believers, now renewed
by the spirit of the New Day, left Badasht
together as they sang the odes that Ṭáhirih had
composed. As they approached the village of
Niyala in Mazandaran, their spectacle proved
too provocative for the locals. Their caravan
was attacked, and they were forced to flee in
different directions.[73]

After the incident of Niyala in August
1848, Bahá'u'lláh and Ṭáhirih, accompanied by
Ṭáhirih's attendant, set out toward Bahá'u'lláh's
home region of Nur in Mazandaran. During this

---

72 Nabíl, 293.
73 Ibid, 299.

time, Ṭáhirih entertained the intention of going to Azarbayjan to meet the Báb. Bahá'u'lláh, however, reminded her of the dangers of such a trip and advised against it.[74]

Ṭáhirih's first stop in Nur was the city of Barfurush, where she stayed at the home of Muhammad Sharí'átmadár, a cleric who was sympathetic to Shaykhísm. Despite the dangers surrounding her, Ṭáhirih began to speak to the public at the same mosque where Sharí'átmadár preached. Once again, the familiar pattern repeated itself. The enthusiasm and devotion shown for Ṭáhirih by the people of Barfurush inflamed the jealousy and wrath of the top Mujtahid in the city, who began to incite his followers against Ṭáhirih. At Sharí'átmadár's suggestion, Ṭáhirih moved to Amul, a nearby city.[75] She then continued her journey through various villages in Mazandaran until she rejoined Bahá'u'lláh in Takur.

Ṭáhirih's overall stay in Mazandaran lasted two years. As a result of the unrelenting efforts by Ṭáhirih's husband, as well as the fierce anti-Bábi posture of the new Prime Minister of Iran, Mírzá Taqí Khan Amír Kabír, Ṭáhirih's whereabouts were

---

74   Mohammad Hoseini, 288.
75   Ibid., 290

finally discovered by government agents in March 1850. She was arrested in the village of Vaz in Mazandaran on the old charges of complicity in the death of her father-in-law and sent to Tehran where she was placed under house arrest at the home of Mahmúd <u>Kh</u>án, the Chief of Police (Kalántar).

Ṭáhirih was imprisoned in a small room on the second floor of a section of the Kalántar's house that had no stair access. There, at the order of Amír Kabír, she was placed under strict watch by agents who were instructed to never allow any pen or paper to reach her. These restrictions, inspired by the authorities' fear of another wave of attraction to Ṭáhirih's presence, did not prevent the flow of her discourse; she managed to establish an ongoing correspondence with many attracted souls, writing on grocery wrapping paper, using broom sticks dipped in green vegetable juice.[76]

Within a short time, the Kalántar's wife and family developed a special affection and deep devotion for Ṭáhirih and began to allow her to accept visitors in other parts of the house. Many influential people in the city, including a large number of Qájár princesses, began to come for visits, and the

---

76   Mohammad Hoseini, 294.

circle of her devotees continued to grow.

Ṭáhirih is reported to have had a meeting with the monarch of Iran, Násiri'd-Dín Shah, just prior to her confinement, during which the Shah offered her clemency if she recanted her beliefs.[77] Another offer of clemency was communicated to Ṭáhirih toward the end of her confinement by the Kalántar:

> I have been given the mission by the
> Prime Minister to tell you that you will
> be taken to Niavaran (the Palace of the
> King) and asked if you are a Bábí. All
> you have to do is to say 'no' and then
> remain silent and in seclusion for some
> time.[78]

In both instances, Ṭáhirih passionately refused, confirming her wish to give up her earthly life for her Beloved.

During Ṭáhirih's confinement, the persecution of the Bábís continued to rage in Iran and more than four thousand Bábís were killed in just one year. Enraged by the vicious killings, a Bábí by the name of Mullá Shaykh-'Alí Turshízí, known as 'Azim, began to promote

---

77   Root, *Ṭáhirih the Pure*, 95.
78   Mohammad Hoseini, 303, Quoting Gobineau, 246-48.

the idea of assassinating the Shah.[79] However, even before 'Azím could develop such a plan, two other Bábís who had come under the influence of his ideas took matters into their own hands and attacked the Shah in a failed attempt that caused him only a slight injury.[80] A great tumult followed this assassination attempt and the gates to the city of Tehran were closed. Already besieged by ongoing persecution, thousands of Bábís-- man, woman, and child-- were massacred in the cruelest of ways.[81] Bahá'u'lláh too was accused of complicity and was imprisoned in the Black Pit.[82]

Although Ṭáhirih was not implicated in this incident, the rising tide of anti-Bábí sentiment among the ecclesiastics and government authorities served to accelerate her martyrdom. Shortly after the assassination attempt, the new Prime Minister, Mírzá Áqá Khán, sent two top mujtahids of Tehran, Mullá 'Alí Kaní and Mullá Muhammad Andarmání, to interrogate Ṭáhirih and do everything in their power to compel her

---

79   Mohammad Hoseini, 309.

80   Ibid, 310.

81   Ibid, 311.

82   The Black Pit, *Síyáh Chál*, was an underground dungeon in Tehran.

to recant her faith. The two mujtahids held seven lengthy meetings with Ṭáhirih, and finding themselves unable to withstand her powerful arguments, ultimately issued a religious judgement (*fatwá*) branding her as a heretic who must be put to death. Ṭáhirih's second meeting with the Shah is reported to have happened shortly after this *fatwá*, when he once again encouraged her to recant her faith in return for clemency. Faced with her firm refusal, the Shah issued a final decree for Ṭáhirih's execution.[83]

Fearful of the consequences of such a news spreading in Tehran, the government devised a plan to execute Ṭáhirih in secret and at night. The exact date of Ṭáhirih's execution is not known, but it is estimated to have happened around the same time as Bahá'u'lláh's imprisonment in the Black Pit in August 1852.

Detailed eyewitness reports by the Kalántar's wife, son, and nephew, as quoted by Nabíl as well as by Mírzá Hasan Adíb and Nicolas, provide a well-corroborated account of the last days of Ṭáhirih's life and her ultimate execution.[84]

Although Ṭáhirih was not told about the verdict, she was intuitively aware of the timing

83   Mohammad Hoseini, 315.
84   Nabíl, 622-29.

and manner of her death. On the day prior to her execution, she met with each one of the female attendants in the house of Kalántar and asked them to forgive her for anything she may have done to offend them. In view of the great love and reverence in which Ṭáhirih was held, these actions bewildered the attendants and brought them to tears. Ṭáhirih then asked the Kalántar's wife not to allow anyone to bring her food or disturb her from that moment on, as she was going to be fasting and praying in preparation to meet her Beloved.[85]

The next day, in the late hours of the evening, the Kalántar, accompanied by another agent, came to take Ṭáhirih to be executed. When Kalántar's wife went to Ṭáhirih's room, she found her perfumed, clothed in white, and adorned with beautiful jewelry. Ṭáhirih gave Kalántar's wife a personal gift and entrusted to her a small box that was to be picked up shortly after her death. Finally, she asked the Kalántar's wife to ask her son to go with her to make sure that her clothes would not be removed prior to her death.

Once outside the house, Ṭáhirih was placed on a horse and her head was covered with the

---

85   Mohammad Hoseini, 326.

Kalántar's cape to keep her from being recognized. On the way to the site of her execution, the Ílkhání garden, Ṭáhirih gave a silk handkerchief to Kalántar's son, asking that it be used for her martyrdom. Upon arrival at the garden, Ṭáhirih was taken to a small room. ʻAzíz khán, the agent in charge, called a Turkish servant of his and gave him the task of executing Ṭáhirih by suffocation. As he approached, Ṭáhirih looked up at him. Awe-struck, the executioner took a few steps back and left the room, unable to carry out the task.[86] A drunken servant was then found to replace the executioner. This time, Ṭáhirih was suffocated with her own handkerchief and her lifeless body was thrown into a ditch in the garden.

According to an eyewitness account written by Dr. Jakob Polak, who claims to have been present, Ṭáhirih endured her execution with "superhuman fortitude."[87]

86   Mohammad Hoseini, 328.
87   Jakob Polak quoted in Momen, *The Bábí and Baháʼí Religions*, 144.

Part 3:
The Discourse of Ṭáhirih

Ṭáhirih's extraordinary heroism has inspired a variety of interpretations about the nature of her significance in human history. In order to gain an accurate understanding of the vision that motivated Ṭáhirih's heroic actions, however, we must examine the contents her discourse.

As a brilliant scholar and a mystic, Ṭáhirih personified the essence of the <u>Shaykh</u>í principle that the ability to grasp the divine will is dependent upon combining spiritual perception with the proof of wisdom. In a treatise written after her recognition of the Báb, Ṭáhirih indicates that in addition to mystical perception her belief in the imminence of a new divine revelation was based on her discernment of changeless divine norms; in particular, the logical expectation that a benevolent God would never leave His creation without guidance or the means to fulfill the purpose of its existence. Ṭáhirih goes on to praise God's unceasing revelation of truth to humanity in these words:

> Day after day the cycle of universe is
> in progress and 'there is no suspension
> in this   emanation.' Praise be to God
> . . . that the cause is everlasting.[88]

In addition to many scholarly treatises, Ṭáhirih's writings consist of a large number of poems, much of which has been discovered and translated only recently during the first decade of the 21st century.[89] Although it is surmised that many of Ṭáhirih's treatises and poems were lost or destroyed after her death, enough of her writings have survived to enable us to gain valuable insights into her discourse.

At the macro level of analysis, Ṭáhirih's poetic discourse may be characterized in its entirety as an exquisite celebration of the progressive revelation of divine truth to humanity

---

88 Quoted in Amanat, *Resurrection and Renewal*, 303.
89 See Hatcher and Hemmat, *Adam's Wish*, 2008; and *The Quickening*, 2011.

and a rapturous proclamation of the advent of the Báb and Bahá'u'lláh as the inaugurators of the Day of Resurrection.

Rich with symbolic allusions rooted in Súfí, Shaykhí, and Islamic thought, and unique in its unmatched mastery of hermeneutics, theology, and philosophy, Ṭáhirih's poetic discourse reflects a deep spiritual understanding of the Revelation of the Báb and a visionary grasp of the station of Bahá'u'lláh.

Given that a full analysis of Ṭáhirih's poetic discourse is beyond the scope of this book, we will place the primary focus of our discussion on Ṭáhirih's prolific use of the symbolism of the "veil" as it relates to the theme of progressive unveiling of divine secrets. In addition, in view of the close connections between key concepts in Ṭáhirih's discourse and the writings of the Báb and Bahá'u'lláh, we will begin our analysis with a brief overview of the relevant themes in the Bábí and Bahá'í writings.

The doctrine of progressive revelation of divine truth-- an overarching theme in the writings of Ṭáhirih-- is central to the teachings of the Báb. The Báb's teachings set forth a completely new perspective on the dynamics of divine revelation in the context of which all religions throughout history are viewed as "products of the interaction between divine effulgence and the receptivity of human beings."[90] In this interactive process, fresh emanations of divine truth are progressively vouch-safed to human beings as their receptive capacities evolve. Given that both the human potential and divine truth are infinite, this mutual interaction is perpetual and unending.[91]

It is important to note that the doctrine of progressive revelation rests on an axiomatic assumption regarding the purpose of creation itself. This assumption is reflected, for example, in an Islamic tradition in the context of which God speaks to humanity in these words: "I was a Hidden Treasure. I wished to be made known, and thus I called creation into being in order that I might be known."[92]

The same emphasis on attainment to the knowledge of God as the primary purpose of human existence is present throughout the writings of the Báb and is affirmed in the writings of Bahá'u'lláh:

> Lauded be Thy name, O Lord my God!
> I testify that Thou wast a hidden Trea-

---

90   Saiedi, 242.

91   Ibid.

92   This is a well-known Islamic Tradition.

sure wrapped within Thine immemorial
Being and an impenetrable Mystery
enshrined in Thine own Essence. Wishing to reveal Thyself, Thou didst call
into being the Greater and the Lesser
Worlds, and didst choose Man above
all Thy creatures, and didst make Him
a sign of both of these worlds, . . . Thou
didst enable Him to unravel Thy mysteries, and to shine with the lights of
Thine inspiration and Thy Revelation,
and to manifest Thy names and Thine
attributes.[93]

Thus, the primary reason for the progressive revelation of divine truth to humanity is
to fulfill the purpose of creation. Wishing to be
known, God created human beings in His image
and bestowed upon them the innate capacity to
unravel His mysteries and manifest His attributes. However, because God is an "impenetrable
Mystery," this purpose must be fulfilled through
intermediaries; the Manifestations of God who
are the direct recipients of divine revelation and
have the mission to educate humanity in the forward march toward the ultimate fulfilment of its

---

93   Bahá'u'lláh, *Prayers and Meditations*, 48.

destiny to attain to the knowledge of God.

As we have seen, another concept central to the process of progressive revelation is the perpetual interaction between humanity's level of receptivity and the outpouring of divine effulgence. Divine truth must be revealed progressively and in accordance with the growing capacity of human beings; because were God to manifest Himself in His full Glory, humanity would be dumbfounded. Therefore, the gradual progression in the removal of the veils that conceal spiritual secrets represents an act of divine compassion.

Ultimately, however, all Manifestations of God throughout history have prophesied about a Day when humanity will meet its Lord face to face. Variously known as the Day of Resurrection, the Day of Judgement, and the End Times, this advent has also come to be known as the "Apocalypse."

It is not surprising that the Greek word "apocalypse," which means "to lift the veil," has come to be associated with a catastrophic end to the world, and that an ultimate revelation of the divine truth on the Day of Resurrection is depicted in terms that denote unprecedented turmoil and upheaval. When the veil is fully lifted, many will not be able to bear its implications; because the complete transformation in the existing norms and structures will "end" the world as they know it.

Hence, the process of divine revelation has been one of gradual unveiling of divine truth to humanity and has involved an ongoing juxtaposition of concealment and revelation. This gradual process is also present in the way that the Báb and Bahá'u'lláh revealed their missions. As such, the symbolism of the "veil" as an object of concealment and revelation is a key motif throughout their writings.

Given that a full analysis of these writings is beyond the scope of this book, we will explore selected illustrations.

As previously discussed, the Báb revealed his mission in stages. In His early writings, He appeared to be identifying Himself as the Gate to the Hidden Imám. He also initially instructed the Letters of the Living to introduce His Cause in the same terms.[94] Upon arriving in the prison of Maku in 1847, however, "He began to proclaim His station to be that of the Hidden Imám, a new Prophet, and ultimately, the Manifestation of the Primal Will

---

94   Nabíl, 84.

of God."[95] As such, the entire ministry of the Báb involved a *gradual unveiling* of His true station and mission, and the symbolism of the "veil" itself was prominently present in His writings.

The association between the process of attainment to the truth and the symbolic removal of the "veil" is notable in the Báb's interpretation of the Tradition of Truth (Tradition of Kumayl). According to this well-known Islamic tradition, one day a disciple by the name of Kumayl put the following question to Imám 'Alí: "O my Lord! What is the truth?" The sequence of statements by Imám 'Alí in response to Kumayl's repeated requests for further clarification are as follows:

> Pierce the veils of glory with no allusion.[96]

> Efface the vain imaginings and confirm the Supreme Object of knowledge.

> Rend asunder the veil for the ascendancy of the Mystery.

> Be thou attracted by the rapture of Absolute Unity unto the Divine attribute of Oneness.

---

95   Saiedi, 19.

96   Another translation for "with no allusion" is "unaided."

Behold, a light hath shone forth out of the Morn of eternity, and lo! Its waves have penetrated the inmost reality of all [Temples of Unity].[97]

These statements convey the same meaning in different ways. They indicate that the seeker of the truth must pierce the veils of glory independently and unaided and rend asunder the veils of vain imaginings until he beholds the light of truth.

Regarding the relationship between the Tradition of Truth and the chronology of the Báb's Revelation, Saiedi states that the Báb's interpretation of this Tradition indicates that,

His entire mission itself is the realization of the Tradition of Kumayl. The first five statements on truth symbolize the first five years, when His truth was divulged gradually.[98]

At the macro level of analysis, two primary meanings are associated with the symbolism of the "veil" in the Báb's writings. The first is the veil that lovingly conceals the divine truth until humanity is ready for its revelation,

---

97   Saiedi, 165-66.
98   Ibid., 169.

while the second is that which prevents human beings from seeking and finding the truth. This latter meaning includes the veils that people *choose* to shut themselves out with, even after a divine truth has been revealed to them. The following are select excerpts that exemplify the symbolic use of the "veil" in the writings of the Báb:

> Were I to remove the veil, all would recognize Me as their Best Beloved.[99]

> Erelong the veil shall be lifted from your eyes at the appointed time.[100]

> I now intend to lift the veil. . . The inception of the year 1260 was the beginning of the revelation of my 'mystery.'[101]

> O ye people of the Bayán! We verily have revealed unto you the knowledge of the exalted station of your being, which lieth in the words of your Lord, that ye may not, in truth, be veiled from Him Whom God shall assuredly

---

99   *Selections from the Writings of the Báb*, 15.
100   Ibid, 46.
101   Saiedi, 129.

make manifest in the Day of Resurrection.[102]

Verily God hath generated within thyself all that He hath fashioned in creation in His likeness, that thou mayest not be veiled from any effulgence.[103]

O congregation of the Bayán. . .! Suffer not yourselves to be shut out as a veil from God after He hath revealed Himself.[104]

None of these did in truth profit thee . . . inasmuch as thou didst veil thyself from God and tarried behind at the time of His manifestation.[105]

The imagery of the "veil" is used in a similar manner, though with some added nuances, in the writings of Bahá'u'lláh. The *Book of Certitude*, revealed during the years prior to Bahá'u'lláh's public proclamation of His mission, which occurred on the eve of His departure from Baghdad, is almost entirely dedicated

---

102 *Persian Bayán*, 1:1, quoted in Saiedi.
103 "Fi's-Sulúk II" Collection, 461, quoted in Saiedi, 59.
104 *Selections from the Writings of the Báb*, 167.
105 Ibid., 32.

to elaborating on the doctrine of progressive revelation and contains repeated references to the imagery of the "veil."

In reference to the advent of the Báb, Bahá'u'lláh states:

> No sooner had that eternal Beauty revealed Himself in Shiraz, in the year sixty, and rent asunder the veil of concealment, than the signs of the ascendancy. . . emanating from that Essence of Essences. . . were manifest in every land.[106]

In the *Book of Certitude*, Bahá'u'lláh draws briefly upon the Tradition of Truth (Kumayl) and presents a new interpretation of the term, "veils of glory," mentioned in that tradition. In this interpretation, He implicates the ecclesiastical authorities of each age as acting as "veils" that intentionally obfuscate the light of divine truth and prevent their followers from attaining to it:[107]

> Among these 'veils of glory' are the divines who, because of their want of discernment and their love and eager-

---

106 Bahá'u'lláh, *The Book of Certitude*, 234.
107 Buck, *Symbol and Secret*, 85.

ness for leadership, have failed to submit to the Cause of God.[108]

The *Book of Certitude* also contains allusions to Bahá'u'lláh's own veiled station during the years in Baghdad in these words:

> Say: O people of the earth! . . . 'Lo:
> The Lamp of God is shining,' and
> summoning you to heed His cause,
> which, though hidden beneath the
> veils of ancient splendor, shineth in
> the land of Iraq above the dayspring of
> eternal holiness.[109]

In one of His Tablets revealed in Adrianople, Bahá'u'lláh indicates that even after his proclamation in Baghdad, the full measure of His Revelation had not yet been revealed:

> Know verily that the veil hiding our
> countenance hath not been completely
> lifted. We have revealed Our Self to a
> degree corresponding to the capacity
> of the people of Our age. Should the
> Ancient Beauty be unveiled in the full-
> ness of His glory mortal eyes would

108   Bahá'u'lláh, *The Book of Certitude*, 164.
109   Ibid, 171-72.

be blinded by the dazzling intensity of His revelation.[110]

In the *Most Holy Book*, Bahá'u'lláh continues to emphasize the progressive nature of His own revelation: "I swear by God, were We to lift the veil, ye would be dumbfounded."[111] At the same time, He asks His followers to endeavor to remove the veils of their vain imaginings: "Burn ye away the veils with the fire of My love, and dispel ye the mists of vain imaginings."[112]

In their 2019 article, "Bahá'u'lláh's Symbolic Use of the Veiled Húríyyih," Hatcher and Hemmat provide a detailed account of the symbolic references to the veiling and unveiling of the Maid of Heaven -- the personification of the Most Great Spirit and of Bahá'u'lláh Himself-- in relation to the various stages of Bahá'u'lláh's Revelation.[113] For

---

110 Quoted in Shoghi Effendi, *The World Order of Bahá'u'lláh*, 117.
111 Bahá'u'lláh, *The Most Holy Book*, 176. Also see Buck, p. 72, for a broader discussion, where the author points out that a "deliberate apposition of manifestation and concealment [is] a recurrent theme throughout Bahá'u'lláh's writings."
112 Ibid., 66.
113 Hatcher and Hemmat, "Bahá'u'lláh's Symbolic Use of the Veiled Hurriyyih," 19.

example, in His poem, "Ode of the Dove," revealed during His seclusion in the mountains of Kurdistan, Bahá'u'lláh employs the symbol of the veil as that which serves to conceal the Beloved until the appointed time of His revelation. In this Ode, the Maiden reminds Bahá'u'lláh that He should not reveal the complete reality about Himself, because if He does so prematurely, the totality of existence will vanish.[114]

In another Tablet, Bahá'u'lláh refers to the veiled Maid of Heaven, who is a reflection of Himself, in these words:

> Cry out before the gaze of the dwellers
> of heaven and of earth: I am the Maid
> of Heaven, the Offspring begotten by
> the Spirit of Baha. . . I was wrapped
> within the veil of an inviolable secu-
> rity and lay hidden from the eyes of
> men.[115]

And, again, in another Tablet He refers to the same concept of inaccessibility of the Most Great Spirit behind the "veils of light:"

---

114 Ibid., 20.
115 Bahá'u'lláh, *Gleanings* 129:10.

> At the time when We were hidden
> behind countless veils of light, thou
> didst commune with Me and didst
> witness the luminaries of the heaven
> of My wisdom. . .[116]

In the *Mathnaví* of Bahá'u'lláh, revealed in Constantinople when the majority of the Bábís were still unaware of His true station,[117] Bahá'u'lláh makes repeated references to the symbolism of the "veil" and the advent of its removal from the Countenance of God, intimating the imminent unveiling of His own station.[118]

Finally, in the *Kitáb-i-Aqdas*, Bahá'u'lláh invites human beings to remove the veils that shut them out from recognizing Him, as exemplified in the brief excerpts below:

> Take heed lest pride deter you from
> recognizing the Source of Revelation;
> lest the things of this world shut you
> out as by a veil from Him who is the

---

116 Bahá'u'lláh, *Tablets*, 143.
117 At that point, a clear separation between Bahá'u'lláh and His half-brother, Yahya, had not yet taken place.
118 Hatcher and Hemmat, "Bahá'u'lláh's Symbolic Use of the Veiled Húrríyyih," 24.

Creator of heaven.[119]

Behold how ye have allowed your learning to shut you out, as by a veil, from Him
who is the Dayspring of this Light.[120]

As already mentioned, the unceasing process of
divine revelation as the primary force in human
progress constitutes the overarching theme in the
discourse of Ṭáhirih. In addition, her use of the
symbolism of the "veil" to expound on the corre-
sponding concepts of concealment and manifestation of the Divine Beloved is in full harmony
with the symbolic meaning of the "veil" in the
writings of the Báb and Bahá'u'lláh.

I will dedicate the following pages to high-
lighting the use of the imagery of the "veil" in
the poetry of Ṭáhirih as that which conceals the
Face of the Divine Beloved, based on selected
excerpts from an unpublished handwritten manuscript that contains a total of approximately
2,200 couplets of her poetry.[121] The 165 couplets

---

119 Bahá'u'lláh, *Kitáb-i-Aqdas*.

120 Ibid.

121 I was very fortunate to obtain three sets of unpublished
handwritten manuscripts attributed to Ṭáhirih from Denis
MacEoin in 1992. He had copied these manuscripts from
the collections available at the National Archives of Iran
during a trip to Tehran in 1977 (prior to the destruction

I have selected and translated for publication in this book represent a fraction of the poems contained in that manuscript. The page numbers listed next to each excerpt correspond to the page numbers of the handwritten manuscript.

---

of the Archives in the course of the 1979 Iranian Revolution). I obtained these manuscripts as a result of a far and wide search for Ṭáhirih's writings in 1992 with the intent to write a book chapter about her life and discourse. It was the insights I gleaned from reading those manuscripts firsthand that ultimately set me on the course to write this book. Note: All three manuscripts were subsequently forwarded to the Bahá'í World Center. The poems contained in two of these manuscripts, obtained through other means, have already been translated and published by Hatcher and Hemmat in their collections of Ṭáhirih's unknown poetry, *Adams's Wish*, 2008 and *The Quickening*, 2011. All three of the above-mentioned manuscripts are considered by experts to be authentic. In addition, the styles, themes, and symbolic references across these manuscripts are consistent and reflect a cohesive discourse.

Excerpt 1 (P. 16)

O thou who by the dawning of Your
almighty beauty
have burned down the sacred veils in
their entirety.

. . .

O thou glorious Almighty Lord
Now nothing remains, be it a speck of dust,

from the veils in the realms of glory,
from the planes of ancestral secrets,

from the sublime veils of *Bahá*,
from the ornaments of praise.

Now burned by the power of the blaz-
ing fire,
nothing remains except the Face of the
Glorious One.

O thou the Most Exalted Lord, O thou
the Most Glorious Lord of the *Bayán,*
[I behold with awe] this Face that
has dawned from the realm of kingly
secret.

Excerpt 2 (P. 21)

Praised be God, He has removed the
veil from His Face,
and has appeared in His dawning
place without concealment.

. . .

O God, He has appeared in clear view,
O God, that Hidden Secret;
verily the secret of wonderment.

. . .

O God, I behold His beauteous Face,
as it shines through adornments and
veils.

Praise be to the power of the Creator,
for He has appeared without veils and
concealments.

Excerpt 3 (P. 41)

The secret of existence veiled him,
and at that moment God appeared to
him in veils.

. . .

Until the assistance of the Beauteous
Beloved reached him,
coming down from the realms of the
Majestic One.

It burned down the veils of his deeds,
It drained all measures of his selfhood.

Excerpt 4, (P. 46-50)

Bring out the secrets from behind the
veils.
Make manifest that which is in concealment.

. . .

The divine effulgence that is concealed in ornaments of light,
do Thou make known by the dawning
of Thy Revelation!

The fiery word that was concealed
and was veiled in its identity as fire,

. . .

It is the Face of God that with might
and dignity
has appeared from behind the veils of
splendor.

. . .

The glorious sun came into the sky,
so that it may discover the secrets.

. . .

Then it concealed its face and hid
itself

behind the shimmering veil of the placeless.

. . .

Where then will the sun of unity dawn from?
Where will the secret of unity shine forth?

. . .

How long will You be veiled in your veils?
How long will You close with one gate hundreds of your gates?

You are the one who devised the plan of separation
and veiled Yourself from us.

. . .

Hear ye My resolute Cause has appeared!
The binding law has become a victorious sign.

Take off the garment of limitations and shackles.
Immerse yourself in the sea of grace.

Excerpt 5 (P. 51)

The hidden Face that was under the
mantle of *Bahá*,
The ecstasy of reunion that was
behind the attire of praise,

has now dawned from the heights of
innamá[122]
and has removed the veils and
[revealed] the secrets.

. . .

The peerless effulgence of Ahmad
is shining from behind the eternal veil.

. . .

The people of this world are veiled
from this secret.
They are bewildered in the turmoil of
their injured hearts.

---

122 This Arabic term means "verily those who," and is a reference to the Qur'ánic verse, 48:10, "Verily those who
were swearing allegiance to you, were indeed swearing
allegiance to Alláh." Here, Ṭáhirih asserts that allegiance
to the new Manifestation equals allegiance to God.

The veils of glory have now been
removed.
Behold, the Beauty has now been
revealed!

Excerpt 6 (P. 53)

The One who with one glorious manifestation
has annihilated all else other than
Him,

He has removed the state of separation
from us
and has sown the seeds of "all are
enriched" throughout creation.

. . .

The soul of Ahmad established itself
in the body.
World upon world was exhilarated by
this joyful announcement.

His station is that of the Most Glorious
Lord, the Most Exalted Lord.[123]
The Greatest Lord of the Garden of
Paradise.

---

123 The Most Exalted, "*A 'lá*," is a descriptor for the Báb.

Excerpt 7 (P. 56)

O pen arise with fervor and zeal.
Pour into tablets the secrets of divine
destiny.

. . .

Speak of the irrevocable verses of
God.
Bring out the secrets from behind the
veil.

. . .

So that everyone may find the Hidden
Secret,
and become aware of the mysteries of
divine destiny.

. . .

Speak of the Hidden Secret that is
concealed,
so that the mysteries of "Be and it
is"[124] may be revealed.

---

124 This is a Qur'ánic reference to the beginning of creation.

Excerpt 8 (P. 57-63)

Whoever recognized that which is in
the *Bayán*,
found the secret of unity from the
manifest Lord.

He beheld mysteries upon mysteries.
He heard so many secrets and songs.
. . .

Any of the levels of the station of
Bahá
at which His Face shines forth,

will illuminate the earth by His dawning.
Worlds upon worlds will shine with
His glory.
. . .

It is as if the Face of God is manifest!
It is as if the call of purity is reverber-
ating.

Excerpt 9 (P. 64)

The secret of the Beloved is openly
visible.

The stranger is no more; no longer can
there be a rival.

He will draw out from His sleeve
the magnetic essence of the Lord of
the Worlds.

. . .

So that they may be accepted by the
Creator
and openly find the hidden secret.

The mystery of creation has become
apparent and evident
from the realms of the Cause of the
now visible Beloved.

Excerpt 10 (P. 66)

Begin to warble your song, O bird of
'Amá[125]
Set aflame the pages of praise.

Speak of the eternal secrets;
Of the unique mysteries yet hidden.

Bring out from behind the veil the face
of *Bahá*.
Strike unconscious by its attraction all
else except Him!
. . .

Bring humanity back to paradise,
and to the station of true greatness
once again.

Make visible the Point hidden under
veils of light
with the signs of your revelation.

---

125 This word can be translated literally as "clouds." However, in a mystical context, it has multiple meanings. It
can refer to the transparent barrier that separates God from
the rest of His creation or be understood as denoting the
divine realm.

Excerpt 11 (P. 67-68)

It is as if the secret of unity has been
revealed,
and the remembrance of "thou shall
not see me" is in our midst.

He rose aloft with shimmering veils.
The hidden unapproachable Face has
dawned!
. . .

Is this the Promised Day or the visible
secret
that has appeared from the station of
the Placeless?
. . .

This is that same luminous lamp,
the light of which bestows the body
with spirit.

The one reflected in the mirror of
Bahá
in the treasury of mysteries, hidden
under the veils.

Excerpt 12 (P. 69)

With thousands of glorious appearances;
with the emanations of His limitless
and infinite favor,

He removed the veil from His Face![126]

The hidden secret has now been revealed.
It has come out from behind the veil
of Divine Oneness.

---

126 This couplet does not have a second line in the manuscript; it is left blank.

Excerpt 13 (P. 71)

Reveal your unseen attraction.
Express your hidden Point.[127]

Transform into peace and reconcilia-
tion
the disagreement you had with us.

Your emanations will not cease, they
will not cease.
Your command will not be delayed, it
will not be delayed.

You have been veiled by Your veils.
You have closed hundreds of Your
gates with one gate.

You Yourself designed this separation,
and veiled yourself from us.

---

127 The "Point" is a reference to the Báb, as in the Primal
Point.

Excerpt 14 (P. 72)

I am the blessed heavenly bird.
I appear from the realms of might.

I will warble the song of the revealed
secret.
I will present myself in the manner of
a king.

Excerpt 15 (P. 73-76)

If the dawning sign were to come out
from behind the veil,
it would burn down all existence with
its brands of fire.

. . .

O God remove the darkness of the
veils,
so that the visage of the brilliant sun
may appear.

O God bring the truth of this beauteous Countenance
out from behind the veil, praised be
Thy Benevolence!

. . .

O God, O Creator, do reveal openly,
Your truth and Your secret.

Excerpt 16, (P. 81)

He who was concealed under the veils,
and [whose concealment] was the
cause of loss from every side,

. . .

Now behold! That secret of creation
has become manifest
in all created things with the ecstasy of
Túr.[128]

Then behold again and see without a
veil,
the signs shimmering through the veil.

---

128 This is a reference to the burning bush on Mount Sinai,
where Moses was struck unconscious by beholding the
divine light.

Excerpt 17 (P. 83)

Praise is shining from the adornments
of *Bahá*.
Praise is dawning from the Face of the
Most Exalted One.[129]

The attributes of God have appeared
in this age;
the ones shimmering and shining since
eternity.

---

129 This is the translation for "*A'lá,*" a reference to the Báb.

Excerpt 18 (P. 84)

That hidden brilliance has become
manifest, how befitting it is!
That Original Point is now proclaimed.
How befitting it is!

. . .

O hearer of Divine verses, take away
this veil that conceals. How befitting
it is!

So that you may see clearly that hidden
effulgence
which has now revealed its face from
behind the veil. How befitting it is!

Excerpt 19 (P. 84)

Take up the pen, O enchanting reed of
Rumi.
Pour out the lines that are made of the
lights of *Párán*.[130]

Speak with your eternal voice about
the secrets.
Remove from the radiant mirror of
proofs

the specks of dust that are veiled from
the hidden effulgence of the Benevolent Lord.

. . .

Pour out your sweetness, O bird of
holiness.
Behold the unveiled Face shining from
the concealed realm.

---

130 This is the name of a mountain range near Mount Sinai
and evokes associations with God revealing Himself to
His Prophets similar to the term, *"Túr."*

Excerpt 20 (P. 85)

O Thou of the station that is above all
stations.
O Thou Creator of the Word that is
above all words.

Cast Thou a glance by Your hidden
grace.
Pour out a drop of that which is Your
perpetual design.

So that this Eternal Point can be made
manifest
without cover, without veil; Singular
is His name.

Excerpt 21 (P. 86)

O God, how is it that the world has
appeared anew?
The horizon is full of light and illumi-
nation of a fire.

O God, has the hidden Face now
appeared?
For it has stolen away our tranquility
and repose.

. . .

Or the Face of the Desired One has
dawned from '*Amá*
It has burned down the whole of
creation with its fire.

. . .

O God bring to our midst the manifestation of the Beloved.
So that He might remove and wipe
away all our burdens.

Excerpt 22 (P. 88)

O God You are witness to every
present moment of ours.
Our story is beyond all descriptions of
how and why.

Help us with Your generosity so that
we may find our way;
That we may manifest in our words
the secret of our condition.

The secret that was hidden in inner
concealment,
has now come out from behind the
veil; Exalted is Our Beauty.

Excerpt 23 (P. 89)

Behold without a veil the beauteous
Face from *'Amá.*
With the light of His Face, He has
obliterated all else.

. . .

Now, take away the veil from the
handiworks of the Creator.
He is closer to the near ones than their
life vein.

Excerpt 24 (P. 91)

With remembrance of the pure name
of the Living Glorious One, and with
respect,
I will now write this page of beautiful
poems.

I will speak of the exalted splendors of
God.
I will now bring out the hidden from
the segment of time.

. . .

I will speak of the hidden Cause that
was veiled under the veils,
so that I may bring joy and delight to
the heavenly ones with this nourish-
ment.

. . .

So that they may grasp the secret that
has manifested itself to our eyes
without removing the veils, visible in
the attire of the All-knowing Almighty.

Excerpt 25 (P. 95)

Behold the Praised Beauty from
behind the veils of His throne.
Shining and shimmering with light.

. . .

Cast aside your dusty and beclouded
veil.
Remove your veils and see the flaming
fire.

Immerse yourself in the sea of fire
and see that which was behind the
covers.

Excerpt 26 (P. 97)

Come thou seeker of divine suffering.
Ask Him for whatever secrets you
wish to know.

For the Conqueror of Eternity has
opened His doors.
His Face is visible from every door.

The time has come to an end, and the
cycles have passed.
The Divine Secret has been made
manifest by the Fountainhead of
Utterance.

Excerpt 27 (P. 102)

It encircled with ecstasy around the
ways of concealment,
until it soulfully appeared through the
manifestation of the inner secret.

Saying, O people of the world, hear
ye! The Divine Secret has appeared
from the realm of destiny; the beauty
of the Eternal is now manifest!

This is the Day of visitation; He is
visible from the realm of *Innamá;*
The manifestation of God in the world
emerging from the secret of "Be and it
is."

Whoever recognizes His Truth will
belong with Him without a doubt;
Whoever remains veiled from Him
will fall headfirst into the nethermost
fire.

Excerpt 28 (P. 104)

Glance with pure sight behind the
fiery veil.
For by the rule of justice the secret of
certitude has appeared.

. . .

O God, I now see clearly the eternal
secret that has emerged
in the dawning adornments, with
honor and certitude.

Excerpt 29 (P. 104)

Once the eternally intoxicated one
shed his vain imaginings,
He drank unadulterated the pure
waters of inner reality.

He beheld in the dawning Face the
sacred verses of truth
that were hidden under the veils of
concealment with eternal lines.

Excerpt 30 (P. 109-114)

O God, the ecstasy concealed under
the veils has now come.
There is no soul worthy of its
announcement among the souls.

. . .

Blissfully, He has removed all veils,
and revealed all secrets to the dwellers
of *Túr.*

. . .

I am that gleaming fire that was
hidden since ancient eternity.
I am that secret of secrets that was
eternally the ultimate purpose.

. . .

O Almighty God, glance at my condition with the eye of Thine assistance.
Assist me to reveal your Secret at
once!

Excerpt 31 (P. 114)

It is dear to me the adoration of the
One, the Almighty, the Praised.
For except His Face naught remains in
existence.

. . .

It is as if the secret of Resurrection
was disclosed to the world;
The Face of the Desired One appeared
from the inaccessible realm of *Há*.[131]

It is as if a new creation has now
appeared in existence.
It is the most pleasing bell that tolls in
the Most Exalted destination.

It is as if that hidden effulgence has
revealed itself;
From whose fiery beauty the whole
earth will burn down.

---

131 This term can have multiple mystical meanings. Here, it
refers to the Divine realm.

Excerpt 32 (P. 117-118)

If you have the desire and longing for
unity,
If you wish to soar to the heights of
glory,

Free yourself from the old covers of
dust.
Cleanse yourself from all evil sparks.
. . .

Then behold the signs of *Bahá* with
the eye of truth.
Rend asunder the veils of glory.
. . .

After burning all else see the manifestation
emanating from the holy mirrors in
Bahá.

Excerpt 33 (P. 119)

Call upon the God of love at this
moment, O seeker of *Bahá*.
For all the gates of *'Amá* have opened
through the Most Exalted.[132]

God, O God, O God, the Most Powerful Almighty!
Cast a glance by Thy grace and set me
free from all else except Thee.

. . .

So that I may behold this luminous
mirror intoxicated.
And see naught else except your
Beauty that shines from the realms of
Há.

That I may speak of that which you
have bestowed upon creation.
The praise of *Bahá al-Abhá* and
Jamí'u'l-A'lá be upon Thee.[133]

---

132 This couplet refers to *Bahá* and *A'lá*; Bahá'u'lláh and the
Báb, respectively. It also makes direct reference to the
Báb as the Gate to Bahá'u'lláh.

133 Note the reference to the twin Manifestations, *Bahá* and
A'lá, in this verse.

Excerpt 34 (P. 120-21)

Behold, again behold, the Face from
the realm of *'Amá* has emerged.
It is as if the secret of secrets has
sounded its call.

. . .

O nightingale, sing the verses of the
people of remembrance,
to see your Desired One removing the
veils of transcendent might.

Excerpt 35 (P. 123)

With praises of the Almighty God,
I will unleash my tongue and make
sparks fly.

I will speak of the secrets of His
Omnipotence.
I will reveal the secret of His victory!

Excerpt 36 (P. 123-24)

O thou adorned with decorations of
light.
Come out this moment from behind
the veils of light.

Remove all of the veils!
Reveal the secret of the *Báb*.

Come and cast aside aught else.
For the Divine Secret [concealed]
since creation has now appeared.

Excerpt 37 (P. 124-25)

With remembrance of the lifegiving God,
I will surely reveal the Hidden Secret!
. . .

With Thy ecstasy, I will reveal the
secrets.
With Thy justice, I will establish
ultimate justice!
. . .

I will drink from the pure cup with my
soul.
I will now bring out the secret from
the *Bayán*!
. . .

O God, Thou will see me manifestly
in Thy love,
and behold me as I speak the secret of
Thy *Bahá*.
. . .

Enable my words to elevate Thy
remembrance,
until You make manifest the secrets.

Praise and gratitude be to Thee, O God.
Grace is Thine, O my true Lord, *Bahá*.

Excerpt 38 (P. 127)

With praises of the Almighty Beloved,
I shall remove the dust from existence.
I will take away all Satanic tempta-
tions and reveal the open secret.

I will see naught other than my
Beloved as the cause in this world.
I will illuminate the seeing eye by the
light of His command.
. . .

O thou hearer, leave all that you have
in hand except Him,
so that you may find manifest the
secret that is its meaning.
. . .

O Thou Peerless God of glory, power,
and majesty.
It is amply clear to Thee who holds the
secret of our time.

But Your people are ignorant of these
verses of truth.

They have fallen into the station of
remoteness and destroyed their
foundations.

O God, open my tongue to speak of
your remembrance.
So that You may reveal the hidden
unseen secret.

Excerpt 39 (P. 129)

In the manner of the *Bayán* and the
open secret,
I will make manifest the secrets from
"Be and it is."

I will now speak of the hidden secrets,
and will cause aught else to collapse.
. . .

I will remove the veils from every
side,
for the fire is now burning ever more
intensely.

O my God, fulfill my wish,
and allow my prayer to be realized!

Excerpt 40 (P. 130)

O God, I ask of Thee by Your majesty
and glory,
which is full well manifest from the
adornments of the *Bayán*.

Give Thy permission from the depths
of the bounties of light,
for the heaven of revelation to become
manifest.

That He may lift up the veil from His
godly Countenance,
and pull out the sword of His wrath
and annihilate all.[134]

---

134 This is a symbolic reference to the Day of Resurrection.
According to Islamic Traditions, on the Day of Resurrection the Qá'im will unleash His sword and slay the unbelievers until the pool of blood on earth reaches up to the
belly of His horse.

Excerpt 41 (P. 130)

With the remembrance of the Mighty God,
spread your wings now, O blessed
bird.

. . .

Speak openly of the sacred stations.
Speak of the hidden adornments.

Speak of the luminous beauteous
Face.
So that the secret of creation may be
revealed.

. . .

But do not speak of the unseen secret,
until this pen begins its quest.

It will unveil with its ink that which
has been hidden.
It will raise [people] out of their tombs
by its attraction.

Illumined by the holy light of the
Glorious One,
all are engaged in Your praise in secret
remembrance.

Excerpt 42 (P. 131)

Behold! It is a New Day and God is
revealed.
The burning light has appeared in
Párán.

Behold clearly with the eye of truth,
and see Him whom no one has ever
seen.

. . .

He is veiled from all other eyes,
with adornments of glory; how aston-
ishing that is!

. . .

If you open your eyes to it,
you will see at once that the mystery
of the Return is manifest!

You will then see all of the secrets,
that have now been revealed from
behind the veils!

Part 4:
The Station of Ṭáhirih

Ṭáhirih's multifaceted significance in human history is marked by an unprecedented courage in proclaiming new spiritual truths. Born in an orthodox environment that was severely punishing and oppressive of independent seekers of enlightenment, Ṭáhirih epitomized the quintessence of heroic audacity in searching for, recognizing, and ultimately unveiling spiritual truths that were destined to transform humanity.

While Ṭáhirih was fortunate to receive a level of advanced education denied to many in her society, it was her spiritual susceptibilities that set her apart from others who were similarly educated. Beyond her brilliance in grasping complex ideas, it was the openness and courage of her heart that enabled her to become a *true* scholar; to independently investigate the truth and embrace its consequences. When faced with the heartrending choice to submit to the tyranny of the Usúlí mujtahids in her family or to leave everyone and everything behind to continue her spiritual quest for the truth, she chose the latter.

In addition to a profound love for the truth, Ṭáhirih was endowed with the gift of mystical perception. She first recognized the Báb in a dream before His declaration and had a visionary grasp of the station of Bahá'u'lláh years prior to His proclamation. In addition, as her poetic discourse clearly demonstrates, Ṭáhirih had a cogent understanding of the nature of the relationship between the two Revelations. The excerpts below, selected from the collections of Ṭáhirih's poems published by Hatcher and Hemmat, provide an illustration of this fact.

One[135]

O Pen remove all separation from our midst.
By divine command, inscribe the Twin Ecstasies,

---

for the entrancing reed of Rumi is play-
ing
that its melody might attract into our
midst the Twin Bolts of light.

. . .

Resurrection Day has arrived with
calamity at the predestined time,
and the sweetness of a new Cause
flows from the Twin Lines of your
pen.

Two[136]

O melodious Nightingale, return!
Sing to us of thoughts wonderous and
refined.

. . .

Recount all the mysteries of the
Point![137]
Bestow again the good news to all
those bewildered lovers!

---

136 *Adam's Wish*, 41-49.

137 A reference to the Báb, who is also known as the Primal
Point. Note: Hatcher and Hemmat provide rich interpre-
tive commentary in the footnotes of their books regarding
the symbolism in these poems. The relevant footnotes
in this volume have benefitted from the information and
insights provided in those books.

. . .

That Cause concealed in the garments
of glory,
that blessed ecstasy veiled by the robe
of praise,
now has dawned from the constella-
tions of *innamá* [138]
and has caused all covers and veils to
be removed!

. . .

Two images manifesting reflections of
hadd,[139]
two suns assisted by two human
temples![140]

Three[141]

This is the New Day when the Sun of
Truth has become manifest

---

138 A reference to the Qur'ánic verse 48:10; "Verily those
who were swearing allegiance to you, were indeed swearing allegiance to Alláh."

139 This term means "extent of capacity." Here, Ṭáhirih is
alluding to the progressive revelation of divine truth
according to the growing capacity of humanity.

140 Here the phrase, "two human temples," alludes to the Báb
and Bahá'u'lláh.

141 *The Quickening*, 149-151.

This is the clamor of the Quickening
[Resurrection] as prophesied in the
books of the old!

. . .

"O my soul's felicity, I behold (before me)
the Arisen One – the Qá'im, the
Self-Subsistent One – the Qayyúm,
the Able."[142]

. . .

Allah, Allah, the Promised Day prophesied in the books of the past
Has at long last become visible!

Four[143]

O God You who are a witness to all
that has transpired,
Assist me at this very moment, O My
Lord,

. . .

What should I recount, O Creator of
all that has come into being?

---

142 Here, the Qá'im refers to the Báb, and the Qayyúm refers
     to Bahá'u'lláh.
143 *The Quickening*, 30-46.

127

The very act of disclosure [revelation]
causes every created thing to become
consumed.

. . .

O my God, what ecstasy this is,
replete with sedition
As if this were the Day of Reunion,
the Day of Resurrection!

. . .

He then appeared from behind the veil
of veils!
He poured forth authoritative pages of
sublime books.

. . .

O my God, the trumpeter has blown
the trumpet
So that the Promised Day has become
manifest!

When the trumpeters descended from
the heavens,
Souls were solaced and gloriously
filled with delight.

. . .

Allah, Allah, what a commotion, what
a congregation this is!
Allah, Allah, the trumpeter has blown
the trumpet!

All who have been created have
awakened and come out,
milling around, bewildered, but
created anew!

Five[144]

Is this the Promised Day? Has the
mystery of manifestation
unveiled its face, adorned with
resplendent ornaments?

Indeed, from behind the veils
of grandeur
The Face of God has appeared with
honor and nobility!

. . .

Truly, with the first appearance He
made everyone totally unconscious;
then, with the second appearance, He

---

144 *Adam's Wish*, 61-74.

will make everyone conscious from
head to toe.

. . .

The Command of God you witness
appeared from two Commands!
The shade of the shadow was shattered
by the Light!

Ṭáhirih's conviction, reflected in the poems
above, that the Day of Resurrection consisted of
two successive Revelations, one by the Báb and
the other by Bahá'u'lláh, corresponds with the
references in the Qur'án to two successive trumpet blasts on the Day of Resurrection. According
to the Qur'án, the first trumpet blast will cause all
who are in the Heavens and the Earth to expire,
and the second one will cause them to arise.

> And there shall be a blast on the
> trumpet, and all who are in the Heav-
> ens and all who are in the Earth shall
> expire, save those whom God shall
> vouchsafe to live. Then shall there be
> another blast on it and lo! Arising they
> shall gaze around them.

> And the earth shall shine with the light
> her Lord, and the Book shall be set,

and the prophets shall be brought up
and the witnesses and judgement shall
be given between them with equity.[145]

The notion of sounding the trumpets as a means of announcing significant events is not unique to the Qur'án. It also constitutes a recurring motif in the Bible.

And in that day a great trumpet will
be blown, and those who were lost
in the land of Assyria and those who
were driven out to the land of Egypt
will come and worship the Lord on the
holy mountain at Jerusalem.[146]

Blow a trumpet in Zion; sound an alarm
on my holy mountain! Let all the inhab-
itants of the land tremble, for the day of
the Lord is coming; it is near.[147]

Indeed, according to the Bible, a mighty trumpet blast will be sounded on the Day of Resurrection:

Immediately after the tribulation of
those days shall the sun be darkened,

---

145 *Qur'án*, 39: 67-9.

146 Isaiah, 27:13.

147 Joel, 1 2:1.

the moon shall not give its light, and
the stars shall fall from heaven, and the
powers of the heaven shall be shaken.
And . . . they shall see the Son of Man
coming in the clouds of heaven with
power and great glory. And he shall send
his angels with a great sound of a trumpet, and they will gather together His
elect from the four winds, from one end
of heaven to the other.[148]

Behold! I tell you a mystery. We
shall not all sleep, but we shall all be
changed, in a moment, in the twin-
kling of an eye, at the last trumpet. For
the trumpet will sound, and the dead
will be raised imperishable, and we
shall be changed.[149]

For the Lord himself will descend from
heaven with a cry of command, with
the voice of an archangel, and with
the sound of the trumpet of God. And
the dead in Christ will rise first. Then
we who are alive, who are left, will be

---

148 Matthew, 24:29-31.
149 Corinthians, 15:51-52.

caught up together with them in the clouds to meet the Lord in the air, and so we will always be with the Lord.[150]

A close examination of End Time prophecies in the Bible and the Qur'án reveals further similarities in their depictions of the Day of Judgement. These include apocalyptic visions of bloodshed and turmoil, rising of dead bodies, severe punishment of the unbelievers, and the reward of eternal life for the faithful. Also, as noted previously, another important similarity between Christian and Islamic prophecies is their converge on the year 1260 A.H./1844 A.D. as the date for the fulfillment of these prophecies.

In contrast to the catastrophic depictions in Christian and Islamic scriptures, Ṭáhirih envisions the Day of Resurrection as a joyous time of worldwide transformation:

Lovers, O Ye Lovers!
The face of truth has become manifest!
Lo, the veils have at last been removed
Through the power of *Rabbu'l Falaq*,[151]

---

150 Thessalonians, 4:13-18.
151 A Qur'ánic term for God, i.e., "The Lord of the Dawn," which appears in the next verse of the poem.

'The Lord of the Dawn!

Arise, each one of you!
In *Bahá* the face of God can be seen!
Look! See how that face,
bright like sun at daybreak,
shines with compassion and delight!

O ye great ones, the Creator of the
Age
has fashioned the universe into a
paradise!
This must be the Day of Resurrection
when morning light shall drive away
all traces of darksome night.

The time for rectitude has come!
Perversity is in retreat!
Indeed, everything you longed for
–Law, Order, Justice–
has at long last appeared!

True knowledge has unveiled itself.
Ignorance has been banished from our
councils.
Go! Tell the <u>Shaykh</u>s of this age
to arise at once
and revise all their texts!

For ages the world's order
has been turned upside down
through vain imaginings of the
learned.
Now milk shall flow instead of bloodshed
If you but set aright the order of the
world.

For though the King of all kings has
appeared
in the manner and custom of a single
nation,
He will, through the mercy of the
Eternal One,
deliver all the peoples of the world
from their burdens and their bondage.[152]

Thus, Ṭáhirih celebrates the Day of Resurrection as a time of the unveiling of the "face
of God," the regenerative power of which will
lead humanity from perversity to rectitude,
injustice to justice, ignorance to independent
investigation of the truth, bloodshed to peace,
and bondage to deliverance; a day on which
the "King of kings" will deliver "all the peo-

---

152   Hatcher and Hemmat, *The Poetry of Ṭáhirih*, 45-6.

ples of the world" from the shackles of outworn and perverse traditions.[153]

In addition to a clear awareness of her mission as the remover of veils from hidden truths, Ṭáhirih's discourse reflects her understanding of that which needed to be unveiled and that which needed to be concealed. Ṭáhirih was guided in this process not only by her spiritual perception but also her ready access to the writings of the Báb. While outwardly she may have appeared to be going beyond the teachings of the Báb in her bold proclamations, in reality, it was her ability to discern in the writings of the Báb what needed to be disclosed and taught to the Bábis at each stage of the Báb's revelation that guided her at all times in her words and actions.[154]

The harmony between Ṭáhirih's increasingly revolutionary proclamations and actions and the Báb's progressive revelation of the true nature of His message is confirmed by the many letters of unequivocal support written by the Báb, in which He praises Ṭáhirih's leadership and affirms her unique understanding of the circumstances of His Cause.

---

153 Note that in this poem, Ṭáhirih foreshadows the universal character of the revelation born in the land of Iran.

154 MacEoin, 180.

The previously cited letter of support written by the Báb to the Bábís of Kazimayn was not the only letter in which He extolled the special station of Ṭáhirih. In another letter written to Ṭáhirih's brother-in-law, Mullá Muhammad 'Alí, the Báb states:

> She verily, in Mine estimation, is a
> noble leaf who hath purified her heart
> from the defilement of limitations for
> the sake of her Lord. May God bless
> all those who appreciate her station
> and refrain from harming her even to
> the slightest degree. For verily she is
> in this day the pride of her kin and the
> honor of all those who follow her in
> the command of God.[155]

In yet another letter the Báb writes about Ṭáhirih:

> She is the one who believed in her
> Lord and opposed her selfish desires;
> and feared the justice of her Lord and
> awaited the Day of meeting Her Cre-
> ator. . . Verily it would be contrary to

---

155 Provisional translation by this author from a Tablet of the Báb quoted in Mohammad Hoseini, *Hazrat-i-Ṭáhirih*, 212.

My pleasure for anyone to deny her;
and if they hear a pronouncement
from her that their minds are unable to
grasp and their souls unable to under-
stand, leave it in His path until God
will pass judgement through the power
of truth.[156]

And, in yet another tablet the Báb states:

It is not for any of the dwellers in the
abode of justice to refute Ṭáhirih in
her knowledge, for she verily is aware
of the realities of the divine Revelation by the grace of God, and she is
in this day a source of honor for this
host. Whoso causeth any injury to her
person in the Cause has committed a
grievous sin.[157]

In addition to the authority and affirma-
tion bestowed upon her by the Báb, another
unique feature of Ṭáhirih's leadership was her

156 Provisional translation by this author from another Tablet of the Báb quoted in Mohammad Hoseini, *Hazrat-i-
Ṭáhirih*, 212.

157 Provisional translation by this author from a third Tablet of the Báb quoted in Mohammad Hoseini, *Hazrat-i-
Ṭáhirih*, 212.

near access to Bahá'u'lláh and the guidance
and protection she received from Him. As we
have already seen, it was Bahá'u'lláh who rescued Ṭáhirih from the peril facing her in Qazvin
and brought her to his home in Tehran. It was
Bahá'u'lláh who arranged for Ṭáhirih's presence in Badasht and entrusted her with the task
of sounding the Trumpet and removing the veil
from the advent of the Promised One. And, after
the incident of Niyala, it was Bahá'u'lláh who
assisted Ṭáhirih in going into hiding in Mazandaran and ultimately enabled her to join Him in
his hometown of Takur.

In one of His tablets, Bahá'u'lláh refers
to Ṭáhirih's recognition of His station in these
words:

> [There was] the Point of Ecstasy
> Jináb-i-Tá, upon her be the Glory of
> God the Most Glorious. For a long
> time, she was with this Servant and
> would not have bartered a moment of
> her visit with this Servant for the king-
> dom of this world or the next. Indeed,
> she did not wish to be separated from
> me for even a moment, but what
> happened was destined to occur. And

so many were the verses and poems she uttered regarding this wonderous Faith. And among them that mention the *Abhá* Countenance was an ode, one verse of which reads:

"If *Bahá* were to cast away the veil from His face,
A hundred thousand like *Azal* would appear."[158]

Bahá'u'lláh also designated a lengthy tablet of visitation to be recited for Ṭáhirih, in which He enumerates her suffering and praises her lofty station. The brief excerpts below, provisionally translated by this author, provide a glimpse into the contents of that tablet:[159]

How can I make mention of the calamities thou endured, O Crimson Leaf? By God, the leaves of the *Sadratu'l-Muntahá* [The Tree beyond which there is no passing] were shed after thou fell from the Tree of the Cause, and the boughs of the Tree

---

158 Bahá'u'lláh, *Lawh-i-Qarn*, provisional translation quoted in Hatcher and Hemmat, *The Poetry of Ṭáhirih*, 2.

159 The original tablet in Arabic is published in *Hazrat-i-Ṭáhirih*, 336-39.

of Immortality broke off, and the branches of the Lote-Tree of Paradise were dried up, and the hearts of the holy ones bled, and the faces of the chosen ones turned pale, and the hearts of the pious were lacerated in the Garden of Repose, and the Faithful Spirit cried out in the presence of thy Lord, and lamented all that dwell on Earth and in Heaven. . . Thou art the one who, as soon as thou heard the call of God, did not tarry even for a moment, and rushed toward Him detached from all else save Him and believed in Him and His supreme verses, and recognized His Manifestation in His days. . . Thou art the one who wast a stranger in thy homeland and a prisoner in thy house and held far from the Court of Holiness despite thy yearning, and wast prohibited from the Habitation of Nearness despite thy longing . . . Thou art the one who was moved at all times by the breezes of the Will of thy Lord, the All-Merciful, as He wished and desired, and there was no movement or stillness for thee unless it was by His command and leave. Well it is with thee for having dissolved thy will in the Will of thy Creator and thy wish in whatsoever thy Lord hath desired. . . Thou art the one who bore in the path of her Lord that which no handmaiden among those who worship God hath endured . . . O thou pride of men!

'Abdu'l-Bahá, the son of Bahá'u'lláh, pays tribute to Ṭáhirih in the *Memorials of the Faithful*. In one passage, 'Abdu'l-Bahá recalls Ṭáhirih's stay at their house in Tehran during his childhood and provides an important glimpse into Ṭáhirih's discourse, including the need for rending the veils asunder and taking bold action in the path of God.

One day, the great Siyyid Yahyá, surnamed Vahíd, was present there. . . With eloquence and fervor, Vahíd was discoursing on the signs and verses that bore witness to the advent of the new Manifestation. She suddenly interrupted him and, raising her voice, vehemently declared: 'O Yahyá! Let deeds, not words, testify to thy faith, if thou art a

man of true learning. Cease idly repeat-
ing the traditions of the past, for the
day of service, of steadfast action, is
come. Now is the time to show forth the
true signs of God, to rend asunder the
veils of idle fancy, to promote the word
of God, and to sacrifice ourselves in
His path. Let deeds, not words, be our
adorning!'[160]

In the context of a brief account of the Conference of Badasht, furthermore, 'Abdu'l-Bahá
presents an unequivocal confirmation of Ṭáhirih's
station as the Trumpeter of the Day of Resurrection:

Ṭáhirih, with her face unveiled,
stepped from her garden, advancing to
the pavilion of Bahá'u'lláh; and as she
came, she shouted aloud these words:
'The Trumpet is sounding!' she
announced, 'The great Trump is
blown! The universal Advent is now
proclaimed!' . . . In this way, the New
Day was announced, and the Great
Day of Resurrection came to pass.[161]

---

160 'Abdu'l-Bahá,1971:200.
161 Ibid., 198-99.

In *God Passes By*, Shoghi Effendi devotes
many pages to honoring the life and leadership
of Ṭáhirih. The select passages below illustrate
Shoghi Effendi's characterization of the station
of Ṭáhirih as the remover of "the veils" and the
"trumpeter" of the Day of Resurrection:

> A little over four years had elapsed
> since the birth of the Báb's Revelation
> when the trumpet-blast announcing
> the formal extinction of the old, and
> the inauguration of the new Dispen-
> sation was sounded. . . The *trumpeter*
> was a lone woman. . .The call she
> sounded was the death-knell of the
> twelve hundred year old law of Islam.
> . . . *tearing through her fiery words*
> *the veils* guarding the sanctity of the
> ordinances of Islam, [she] sounded the
> clarion-call, and proclaimed the inaugu-
> ration, of a new Dispensation. On that
> memorable day the 'Bugle' mentioned
> in the Qur'án was sounded, the 'stun-
> ning trumpet-blast' was loudly raised,
> and the 'Catastrophe' came to pass.[162]

---

162 *God Passes By*, 33. Italics added.

As these resounding characterizations by the central figures of the Faith for which she sacrificed her life clearly demonstrate, Ṭáhirih's significance in human history goes far beyond the popularized image of her as a woman who broke free from the shackles of gender norms. The vision that animated Ṭáhirih's heroic life and inspired the prolific stream of her discourse was one of an imminent transformation in the human civilization. And the veils that she lifted in Badasht represented the most apocalyptic of the veils she had been divinely ordained to remove from the advent of the Promised One.

References

'Abdu'l-Bahá. *Memorials of the Faithful*, pp. 190-203.

Amanat, Abbas. *Resurrection and Renewal: The Making of the Bábí Movement in Iran*, 1844-1850. Ithaca, NY: Cornell University Press, 1989.

_____. *The Early Years of the Bábí Movement: Background and Development*. Doctoral Dissertation, University of Oxford, 1981.

The Báb. *Selections from the Writings of the Báb*. Wilmette, IL: Baha'i Publishing.

Baghdádí, Muhammad Mustaphá. *Treatise on the Cause,* Cairo: 1919. Digitally republished, East Lansing, Mi.: H-Bahai, 1998.

Bahá'u'lláh. *The Kitab-i-Íqán; The Book of Certitude.* Trans. Shoghi Effendi. Wilmette, IL: Baha'i Publishing, 1950.

_____. *Gleanings from the Writings of Bahá'u'lláh.* Trans. Shoghi Effendi. Wilmette, IL: Baha'i Publishing, 1962.

_____. *The Kitáb-i-Aqdas; Most Holy Book.* Haifa: World Center Publications, 1992.

_____. *Prayers and Meditations.* Bahá'í International Community.

_____. *Summons of the Lord of Hosts.* Bahá'í International Community, 2010.

Balyuzi, Hasan. *The Báb.* Oxford: George Ronald, 1973.

Buck, Christopher. *Symbol and Secret: Qur'an Commentary in Bahá'u'lláh's Kitab-i-Íqán.* Studies in the Bábí and Bahá'í Religions, Volume 7. Los Angeles: Kalimat Press, 1995.

Gobinequ, M. Le Comte De. *Les Religions et les Philosopies dans l'Asie Centrale.* Paris: Ernest Leroux. 1900.

Hatcher, John and Hemmat, Amrollah. *The Poetry of Ṭáhirih.* Oxford: George Ronald, 2002.

_____. *Adam's Wish: Unknown Poetry of Ṭáhirih*. Wilmette, IL: Baha'i Publishing, 2008.

_____. *The Quickening: Unknown Poetry of Ṭáhirih*. Wilmette, IL: Baha'i Publishing, 2011.

_____. "Bahá'u'lláh's Symbolic Use of the Veiled Húríyyih," *The Journal of Baha'i Studies*, 29.3, 2019.

MacEoin, Denis. *From Shakhism to Bábísm: A Study in Charismatic Renewal in Shi'i Islam*. Doctoral Dissertation, King's College, Cambridge, 1979.

Mohammad Hoseini, Nosratollah. *Hazrat-i-Ṭáhirih*. Association for Baha'i Studies in Persian, Dundas, Ontario, 2000.

Momen, Moojan. "Usúlí, Akhbári, Shaykhí, Bábi: The Tribulations of a Qazvin Family." *Iranian Studies*, 36:3, September 2003.

_____. *The Bábí and Bahá'í Religions: Some Contemporary Western Accounts, 1844-1944*. Oxford: George Ronald, 1981.

Nabíl-i-Zarandi. *The Dawn Breakers*. Translated and edited by Shoghi Effendi. Wilmette,

IL: Bahá'í Publishing, 1932/1962.

Nicolas, A.L.M. *Seyyed Ali Mohammad dit Let Báb*. Paris: Dujarric & Company, 1905.

Rafati, Vahid. *The Development of Shaykhí Thought in Shi'i Islam*. Doctoral Dissertation, University of California, Los Angeles, 1979.

Root, Martha. *Ṭáhirih the Pure*. Los Angeles: Kalimat Press, 1981.

Rosen, Harold. *Founders of Faith: The Parallel Lives of God's Messenger*. Wilmette, IL: Baha'i Publishing, 2010.

Saiedi, Nader. *The Gate of the Heart: Understanding the Writings of the Báb*. Canada: Association for Baha'i Studies and Wilfried Laurier University Press, 2008.

Shoghi Effendi. *God Passes By*. Wilmette: Baha'i Publishing. Original publication, 1944.

Samandar Qazvíní, Shaykh Kázim. *Tarikh-i Samandar*. Published in *Tarikh-i Samandar va Mulhaqqát*, A. Ala'i (ed.) 1975.

Smith, Peter. *The Bábí and Bahá'í Religions*. Cambridge: Cambridge University Press, 1987.

About the Author

Dr. Roya Akhavan is currently a Professor at the Department of Mass Communications, St. Cloud State University. She is an award-winning educator and scholar whose research has been published in top international peer-reviewed journals. Dr. Akhavan is a frequent speaker at national and international forums on world peace, social justice, gender equality, and spirituality in the 21st century. Her most recent work includes a book entitled *Peace for Our Planet: A New Approach*. Dr. Akhavan has lived and worked in four different cultures: Persian, American, Japanese, and Chinese. She currently lives in Minneapolis, Minnesota.

Printed in Great Britain
by Amazon

48438960R00091